The Year-Round Gas Barbecue Cookbook

Jo-Anne Bennett

Random House of Canada

Published in 1993 by Random House of Canada Limited, Toronto.

Canadian Cataloguing in Publication Data

Bennett, Jo-Anne, 1952–
The year-round gas barbecue cookbook

Includes index.
ISBN 0-394-22335-7

1. Barbecue cookery.   I. Title.

TX840.B3B45 1993   641.7'6   C93-093287-0

Cover design by Andrew Smith
Cover photograph by Hal Roth Photography Inc.
Text Design by Glenn Ross

FRONT COVER: Sesame Sirloin with Vegetable Kabobs

Printed and bound in Canada

10 9 8 7 6 5 4 3 2 1

To my Mom and Dad,
Earle and Ruth Matthie

My parents introduced me to fine foods, good cooking and an array of unusual dishes at a young age. They made sure that part of my education was learning how to prepare them.

With special thanks to my kitchen helpmates, George, Matthew, Courtney, Joel, Ashley, Drew and Paige Bennett. Wilf and Yvette Bennett were always there when I needed babysitters.

An added thanks to the recipe testers, Keith and Ann Eady, Chris and Theresa Leppan, Charlie and Robynne Eagan, Dave and June Stewart, Graham and Laurie Ditchfield and Jim Gurney.

I am also grateful to my agent, Carol Bonnett, for her belief in me, my editor, Sarah Davies, for her enthusiasm and support, Jim Gurney for finding the door and Pierre Burton for opening the door.

Contents

Introduction 1

Equipment and Safety 5

Appetizers and Beverages 17

Eggs and Breakfast Dishes 47

Beef and Pork 57

Lamb and Poultry 75

Fish and Shellfish 95

Vegetables and Rice 117

Salads and Dressings 151

Sauces 171

Desserts 183

Menu Plans 203

Glossary 207

Index 213

Introduction

Over the last ten years, most people have changed their eating habits significantly. We are moving to lighter foods and cooking methods and experimenting with foods from different countries and regions, such as Thai and Cajun. As we do this we have the added benefit of learning more about our neighbours from other lands.

I urge you to shop the specialty or ethnic markets and ask questions. Most store owners will be more than happy to answer. Try different vegetables, fruits, fish and seasonings. Don't be put off by your children. They may surprise you. I have six children with well-developed palates (I just don't always tell them what they are eating!). We often have the children's friends at our dinner table, and they are fascinated by what we are eating and ask a multitude of questions. One girl told me that even if her mother didn't buy my next cookbook, *she* was going to.

These recipes have been tested and retested and, in all the confusion, I hope we didn't make any errors. There were many evenings, especially towards the end of the book, that I would call the neighbours at the last minute to come and help eat and grade the dishes I had prepared. Sometimes there were as many as fifteen dishes on the table and everyone would taste a little bit of each. I had notes all over the kitchen walls and, as George would bring food in from the barbecue, I would be running to the recipe asking him how long it took to cook and were the grill setting and temperature correct.

We tested all the recipes in winter as well as summer. We discovered that cooking times varied significantly as the temperature ranged from -10° to -30°F (-23° to -35°C). The wind was also a factor in altering cooking times. Consequently, the best I can tell you is that dishes cooked in winter can take 5 or 10 minutes longer, depending on the weather and the dish. A roast, of course, will take much longer.

I encourage you not to put your barbecue away for the winter. You can barbecue in any kind of weather, and there is nothing like a barbecued meal on a dreary winter day to cheer you up and make you think of summer and sunshine.

Don't confine your barbecuing to just meat dishes. You can cook virtually anything on the barbecue that you cook in your oven. One of the nicest advantages is that I can prepare all the food in advance and visit with my friends as the men stand over the barbecue with my husband, offering advice. Of course, since this is the nineties and roles are so often reversed, you and your partner might want to exchange jobs. On hot summer days there is the bonus of not heating up my kitchen by turning on the oven.

The only disadvantage is that I can't seem to teach my husband to bring all of the pans and cooking utensils back to the kitchen and usually find them outside the next day, after the dishes are done!

Here are a few general hints to keep in mind when barbecuing.

- Meat should not be salted before cooking; the salt draws out the juices and toughens the meat.

- Use tongs to turn meat rather than a fork. Puncturing the meat causes it to lose its natural juices.

- Rub salad oil on meat and fish before barbecuing to prevent drying and sticking.

- Rub salad oil on cooking rack to minimize sticking.

- Wooden skewers and string should be soaked in water before using to prevent them from burning.

- When steaming vegetables in foil, place a few ice cubes in the packet, on top of the vegetables, before sealing. They are more manageable than water, and melt gradually to moisten the vegetables.

- If you wish to make gravy with the drippings from a roast, turkey or chicken, position an aluminum pan underneath the meat.

- Trim excess fat from roasts, steaks and chops to avoid flare-ups.

- Remove roasts from the grill when they are 5°F (a couple of degrees C) short of being done. Allow them to rest for 10 minutes before carving. The meat will be easier to slice and will continue to cook slightly during the resting time.

- Do not leave thermometer in meat while cooking. Make sure the thermometer is in the centre of the meat and not touching bone.

- Always preheat your barbecue before cooking. Set burners on High and close the lid for at least 10 minutes.

- Cook with the lid down unless otherwise directed for correct timing.

- Cooking times in recipes are approximate. They can vary according to the temperature, amount of wind and amount or size of food being cooked.

- If your barbecue is designed such that you cannot change the grill settings, adjust the temperature and cooking time.

Equipment and Safety

CHARCOAL VERSUS GAS

Charcoal is odourless and flavourless. The wonderful flavour associated with barbecuing is a result of the juices and fats dripping on the hot charcoal or lava rock. The flare-up and smoking imparts the so-called charcoal flavour to the food you are cooking.

Charcoal is consumed in use. Once ignited, it slowly burns up, reaching a peak of heat output, then gradually burning away to ash. It is then necessary to add new charcoal if continuing to cook for any length of time. Consequently, it is impossible to maintain an even cooking temperature.

The gas grill uses non-combustible volcanic rocks, which never burn up. They are distributed over a rack and are heated in the gas flames. It is easy to set a desired cooking temperature with a gas grill by simply adjusting the flame, and with the constant flame, an even temperature is maintained.

BTUs

The various barbecues on the market have different BTUs (British Thermal Units). This, simply put, is the heat necessary to raise the temperature of one pound of water one degree Fahrenheit. The range can vary from 30,000 to 50,000 BTUs, and portable barbecues usually have about 20,000 BTUs.

The number of BTUs featured on your barbecue will greatly affect the cooking times. With the first barbecue cookbook I wrote, the recipes were tested on a 35,000 BTU barbecue. For this book, they were tested on a 50,000 BTU barbecue. Hence, the changes in the cooking times. The more BTUs, the shorter the cooking time.

Through time and experience, you will get to know your barbecue and be able to make the necessary adjustments.

BASIC
OPERATING INSTRUCTIONS

Lighting Your Grill

1. Raise the lid before lighting.

2. Be sure control knobs are set at Off. Turn on gas supply at tank.

3. Set control knob to High.

4. Quickly push ignitor button a few times. Grill should ignite within 5 seconds. If you do not have an ignitor button, quickly light through the lighting hole with a match or approved gas grill ignitor.

5. With twin-burner barbecues, turn on one side only while lighting. When the first burner is lit, the other side should ignite automatically when you turn on the control knob.

If the burner does not ignite, turn the control knob to Off, wait 5 minutes for the gas to dissipate and try again.

Preheating the Grill

Always preheat the grill before using, with the lid closed. Be sure to raise the lid before lighting, though. Set the control knob on High for 5 to 10 minutes. The grill broils better when the lava rocks are hot because the grease dripping on them flares up and imparts that great barbecue flavour to the meat.

Adjusting the Lid Position

Most gas grills can be operated with the cover completely closed or opened, or at several different levels of partial opening. A closed lid will provide a smokier flavour but, with some foods, you may prefer leaving the lid open slightly to allow excessive smoke to escape. Of course with the lid closed, the food will cook faster and use less gas, and you will be able to maintain cooking temperature.

COOKING METHODS

Indirect Method

The indirect method works much the same way as a convection oven. You operate one burner and place the food over the other. Cooking heat is radiated from the operating burner and surrounds and cooks the food on the other side of the grill. This method is especially effective when you want to cook slowly without the food coming in contact with the flames.

Since the heat is circulating, it is not necessary to turn the food. All preheating and cooking is done with the lid down.

Surface Broiling with Lid Raised

This method of broiling exposes only the bottom side of the meat or food to cooking temperatures. It is the slowest method of cooking on a gas grill and is, therefore, suitable only for foods that cook quickly.

Surface Broiling with Lid Lowered or Closed

Foods cook more quickly when the lid is lowered because heat is confined in the grill and both the top and bottom surfaces of the food are exposed to cooking temperatures.

You will also get more smoky flavour when you cook with the lid lowered as there is more flaming and more smoke. Be careful not to overcook the food, though. When broiling steaks or hamburgers, use a High setting to sear the surface. This will help keep the meat inside moist and juicy, without overcooking the centre of the meat.

Roasting or Baking

By closing the cover of your gas grill you can make it an oven. By means of burner adjustments and the heat indicator, you can control the temperature inside the grill and use it to bake, roast or barbecue an incredible variety of foods.

Rotisserie Broiling

There are several advantages to rotisserie broiling. The meat browns and cooks evenly on all surfaces and does not require constant attention. Whole turkeys, chickens, hams and large roasts can be barbecued with delicious results. Exact degrees of doneness can be easily determined by the use of a meat thermometer.

Insert the spit rod lengthwise through the centre of the meat, balancing it carefully. Secure with holding forks. Roll the spit in the palms of your hands to see if it is balanced. If the weight is not evenly distributed, the spit rod will stop turning once the heavier side of the meat rotates to the down side.

Flare-ups

A reasonable amount of flaming and smoking is desired in broiling or cooking most kinds of meat because that is what produces the barbecue flavour, the essence of outdoor cooking. Of course too much will cause burning and charring of the meat and should be avoided.

To reduce or eliminate flare-ups:

- Trim surplus fat off meat or fowl before cooking.

- Purchase lean cuts of meat, and ground chuck or round for hamburgers.

- Avoid pre-basted turkeys, as they are filled with oil and need careful watching for excessive flare-ups.

- Cook with grids at top level and, if necessary, burner at lower setting.

- Have a squirt bottle of water handy to douse minor flare-ups. Use baking soda for grease fires.

- Flaming can be controlled, in some cases, by adjusting the lid slightly open.

Smoking

Using a covered grill, smoking gives a wonderful added flavour to meat, poultry and fish. Smoking woods are available in chips or chunks. Chunks burn longer than chips and are better for foods with longer cooking times. Wood chips and chunks should be soaked in water for about 30 minutes before using. Place them evenly over the lava rocks, being careful not to smother the fire. Use a handful or two of chips or two or three chunks at a time. The more wood, the stronger the flavour.

Do not use wood that has been commercially treated with chemicals. Softwoods, such as pine, are not recommended, as they give the food a bitter flavour.

- HICKORY: Has a definite "smoked" flavour. Robust and western.

- MESQUITE: Has a lighter "smoked" flavour. More southern in taste.

- APPLE AND CHERRY: Have a more delicate flavour. Excellent with poultry.

- NUT WOODS: Have a milder smoke flavour.

- GRAPEVINE CUTTINGS: Have a subtle sweet flavour.

For additional flavouring, throw some garlic cloves, fresh or dried herbs or fruit rinds on the rocks.

Cooking Times

A cooking time chart is not an exact guide for cooking with a gas barbecue because you will be cooking outdoors where temperatures and wind can influence the rate of cooking. Different barbecues, size of the meat and how often the lid is raised also have an effect on the cooking times.

There is no better way to ensure good cooking results than careful attention to the food on the grill. If you are cooking thick cuts of meat or whole fowl, a meat thermometer is your best insurance of exact cooking results. But be careful, as some meat thermometers, left in while cooking, can give false readings. Your best guide is your own experience in the use of your gas grill. You will soon become an expert in gauging the amount of time needed to cook various foods and meats to the desired degree of doneness.

High Setting (Approximately 550°F/290°C)
Use this setting for searing steaks and chops, for a fast warm-up or for burning food residue from the grills after you are finished cooking. You seldom use this setting for extended cooking.

Medium Setting (Approximately 450°F/230°C)
Use this setting for most grilling, roasting and baking as well as for hamburgers and vegetables.

Low Setting (Approximately 350°F/180°C)
Use this setting for rotisserie cooking and smoking.

(Given temperatures will vary with the outside temperature and the amount of wind.)

Cleaning

Once you are finished cooking, burn off any food residue by setting the control to High, closing the lid and heating for 5 to 10 minutes or until the smoking stops. After turning the heat off, use a long-handled wire brush to clean the grills. Protect your hands with oven mitts.

You do not have to clean your barbecue after every use, but if you wish to give it an occasional scrubbing, use a mild solution of soap and water and rinse thoroughly. Never use a commercial oven cleaner.

For a more thorough cleaning of the grill and briquets, place a large piece of heavy-duty aluminum foil, shiny side down, on top of the cooking grill. Leave gaps on the sides of the grill open so you are covering only three-quarters of the cooking surface. Ignite the grill with the burners on High, close the lid and let heat for 10 minutes. Turn all burners off and let cool. Remove the foil.

PREVENTIVE
MAINTENANCE AND SAFETY

If you smell gas:

1. Shut off gas to appliance.

2. Open grill lid.

3. Extinguish any open flame.

4. If odour continues, immediately call your gas supplier.

WARNING:

Always raise the lid before lighting.
Never bend over the grill when lighting.

If the burner does not ignite:

1. Turn the control knob to Off, wait 5 minutes and try igniting again.

2. Check the gas supply.

3. Check for obstructions in the gas line.

4. Check for spider webs in the venturi tubes (short tubes connecting burner to gas manifold). Plugged venturi tubes prevent the propane from flowing to the burner.

Location and Clearances

If your gas grill is to be close to the house or any other combustible surface, observe and follow the manufacturer's instructions for clearances from combustible materials.

Safety Reminders

- Keep the area around and under the grill free from anything that might obstruct the flow of air for combustion and ventilation.

- Do not install grill under overhead unprotected combustible surfaces! Grills should be outdoors in a well-ventilated space, not in a garage or other enclosed area.

- Do not store or use gasoline or any other flammable vapours or liquids near the barbecue or any other appliance.

- Keep electrical supply cord and gas supply hose away from any heated surface.

- Do not use charcoal in your grill; it will dissipate and plug the holes.

- Do not operate your grill if there is a gas leak. Do not use a match to check for gas leaks. Always use a soap water solution (see Testing for Gas Leaks, page 13).

- Do not disconnect any gas fittings while grill is being used.

- If your barbecue does not ignite immediately, or if the burners go out during use, turn all controls off and wait 5 minutes before attempting to relight.

- Set the grill on a level surface out of traffic paths.

- Keep young children and pets away from barbecue to prevent serious burns.

- As soon as you are finished using the barbecue, turn off the cylinder shut-off valve first and then turn the grill controls to Off. This allows gas in the gas lines to burn off.

- Tighten and check all connections each time the cylinder is filled and reconnected to your barbecue.

- If your tank is rusty or dented, it should be checked by your propane dealer. Propane cylinders are required to be inspected, fitted with a new relief valve and requalified 10 years from date of manufacture.

Testing for Gas Leaks

Check for gas leaks every time you disconnect and reconnect your gas fitting. Once all connections have been made, and valve knob is in the Off position, turn gas on at the cylinder and check for leaks. Never test with a lighted match! Test with a soap water solution. Do not smoke while testing!

To prepare a soapy solution, mix one part dish detergent and one part water. Paint every joint in the pipeline. Bubbles, a hissing sound or an obnoxious odour indicate gas leaks. Turn gas off and tighten any connection that appeared to be leaking. Retest for leaks.

Storing Your Gas Grill

When the grill is to be stored indoors, the cylinder must be disconnected from the grill and stored outdoors in a well-ventilated area.

If the cylinder is not disconnected from the grill, the grill and cylinder must be stored outdoors in a well-ventilated area.

To ensure safety and good performance, all adjustments, servicing and replacement parts (such as burners, valves and regulators) should be handled by your local dealer, gas company or a qualified serviceperson.

EQUIPMENT

Always keep a "spare tire" — a full propane tank. There is nothing worse than running out of gas when you are in the middle of cooking a meal. It also takes the worry out of wondering how much gas is left in the tank.

Rotisserie Basket
The food is held between two wire racks and the unit is mounted on the spit rod. Excellent for fish and poultry parts.

Hinged Grill Basket
They come in a variety of shapes and sizes. Can be used for meat, fish and poultry.

Fish Grill
You never have to worry about delicate fish falling through the grill. Excellent for any small foods. Eliminates the need for aluminum foil in many cases.

Griddle
Used for pancakes, eggs, bacon. A handy accessory.

Long-Handled Tongs
Used for moving and turning foods without piercing. Can also be used for moving lava rocks.

Basting Brushes
Necessary for many recipes. Try to get long-handled ones for safety.

Meat Thermometer
A necessity for testing the doneness of food. Never leave it in the meat while grilling.

Skewers
Long ones are used for kabobs. Short wooden ones are used for seafood and satay. Poultry skewers hold together fish and poultry. Be sure to soak wooden skewers in water for 5 or 10 minutes before using.

Heavy-duty Aluminum Foil
Necessary for many recipes. Use for food that is too small for the grill, to prevent it from falling through the rack. Excellent for delicate fish and vegetables. Can also be used to hold wood chips.

Drip Pans
Disposable aluminum pans that can be used a number of times before being thrown away. Excellent for catching meat juices when using the indirect method of cooking.

Wire Grill Brush
For removing food residue from your grill.

Appetizers
and
Beverages

Pork Satay

This dish is just spicy enough to whet your guests' appetites and have them anxiously await the next course.

1 pound	lean pork	500 g
3 tablespoons	vegetable oil	50 mL
1 tablespoon	thinly sliced lemon grass (or 1 green onion)	15 mL
1 teaspoon	finely chopped red chili pepper	5 mL
2 teaspoons	dark brown sugar	10 mL
1 tablespoon	fish sauce	15 mL

Slice the pork into strips 2 inches (5 cm) long, and place in a bowl.

Place the remaining ingredients in a blender or food processor, and purée. Pour purée over the meat and stir to coat completely. Place in refrigerator to marinate for a couple of hours.

Thread the pork strips onto wooden or bamboo skewers.

Place on the lower grill over medium heat, turning until done on all sides.

Serve with Peanut Sauce (page 182) for dipping.

Cooking Time: 10 minutes

Serves 4

Fish sauce is made from the liquid drained from salted, fermented anchovies. Use sparingly. It is an essential ingredient in the cooking of some Asian countries and can be found in Asian and specialty food stores.

Lime Chicken Satay

2	chicken breasts, boned and skinned	2
1 tablespoon	lime juice	15 mL
1 tablespoon	vegetable oil	15 mL
1 teaspoon	soya sauce	5 mL
1	garlic clove, crushed	1
1 teaspoon	grated lime rind	5 mL
1 teaspoon	sugar	5 mL

Slice the chicken into strips 2 inches (5 cm) long, and place in a bowl.

Mix together the remaining ingredients and add to the chicken. Marinate for 2 hours, stirring occasionally.

Thread the chicken strips onto wooden or bamboo skewers.

Place on the lower grill over medium heat until done on all sides.

Serve with Tzatziki (page 179) for dipping.

Cooking Time: 5 minutes

Serves 4

Curried Chicken Rolls

Curried Chicken Rolls can be prepared in advance and frozen. They are nice to have on hand when unexpected guests drop in.

1 cup	finely chopped cooked chicken	250 mL
1 cup	mayonnaise	250 mL
¾ cup	shredded Monterey Jack cheese	175 mL
⅓ cup	finely chopped almonds	75 mL
¼ cup	chopped fresh parsley	50 mL
1	small onion, minced	1
2 teaspoons	curry powder	10 mL
2 teaspoons	lemon juice	10 mL
½ teaspoon	salt	2 mL
½ teaspoon	pepper	2 mL
18 slices	whole wheat bread	18
¼ cup	butter, melted	50 mL

In a large bowl, combine chicken, mayonnaise, cheese, almonds, parsley, onion, curry, lemon juice, salt and pepper. Blend well. Cover and refrigerate for 30 minutes.

Trim crusts from bread and flatten slices with a rolling pin. Spread about 2 tablespoons (25 mL) chicken mixture on each slice and roll up. Cut each roll in half and secure with toothpick. Place on baking sheet or griddle, seam side down, and brush with melted butter.

Place on upper grill over medium heat, with lid down.

Cooking Time: 8 minutes

Remove toothpicks before serving. For a little added flavour and colour, lay a piece of fresh dillweed on top of each roll before serving.

Makes 36 rolls

Soft Shell Crabs with Seasoned Mustard Baste

These are so tender and succulent, they will literally melt in your mouth and you'll have trouble differentiating the meat from the shell.

6	soft shell crabs	6
2 tablespoons	melted butter	25 mL
2 tablespoons	olive oil	25 mL
1	garlic clove, crushed	1
1 tablespoon	lemon juice	15 mL
2 tablespoons	chopped fresh parsley	25 mL
2 teaspoons	Dijon mustard	10 mL
½ teaspoon	salt	2 mL
¼ teaspoon	pepper	1 mL

Prepare the crabs: Pull away the triangular piece on the underside (apron). Turn over and keep pulling, removing the top shell. Trim off the "devil's fingers" or spongy gills from each side of the top of the crab. Discard the internal organs, the mouth and the appendages at the front.

Mix together the remaining ingredients for the baste.

Place the crabs on the upper grill over medium heat, basting with the sauce frequently.

Cooking Time: 5 minutes

Serves 6

Oysters Rockefeller

When we go out for dinner, if Oysters Rockefeller is on the menu, my husband doesn't bother to ask what I am having for an appetizer. I had to develop a recipe so I could have it more often.

24	fresh oysters	24
	Rock salt	
¼ cup	butter	50 mL
1	small onion, finely chopped	1
1	garlic clove, minced	1
1 tablespoon	chopped fresh parsley	15 mL
1 pound	cleaned spinach, chopped	500 g
Dash	hot pepper sauce	Dash
½ teaspoon	salt	2 mL
¼ teaspoon	pepper	1 mL
1 teaspoon	Pernod or Anisette (optional)	5 mL
3 tablespoons	whipping cream	50 mL
¼ cup	dried bread crumbs	50 mL

Wash the oysters and open the shell with an oyster knife. Remove oysters and drain off the juice. Save half of the shells. Return the oysters to the half shell. Line a shallow pan with rock salt to keep shells steady and arrange the oysters on top. Set aside.

In a saucepan, melt the butter. Sauté the onion and garlic for 1 minute. Add the remaining ingredients and cook and stir over low heat for 5 minutes. Place mixture in food processor or blender and process until smooth. Top each oyster with a tablespoonful of the spinach mixture.

Place pan on the upper grill over medium heat until topping is lightly browned. Serve immediately.

Cooking Time: 10 minutes

Serves 6

HINT: When buying oysters in the shell, pick ones with the shells tightly closed. Shucked oysters should be plump, shiny and fresh smelling.

Oysters Bienville

If you like Cajun food, this dish will make you feel like you're in New Orleans.

24	fresh oysters	24
	Rock salt	
4	strips bacon, chopped	4
3 tablespoons	butter	50 mL
½ cup	chopped onions	125 mL
2	garlic cloves, minced	2
⅓ cup	flour	75 mL
½ teaspoon	salt	2 mL
¼ teaspoon	black pepper	1 mL
½ teaspoon	paprika	2 mL
Pinch	cayenne pepper	Pinch
¼ teaspoon	dried thyme	1 mL
1 cup	chicken broth	250 mL
½ cup	whipping cream	125 mL
3	egg yolks, beaten	3
½ pound	cooked shrimp	250 g
½ cup	finely chopped mushrooms	125 mL
3 tablespoons	dry white wine	50 mL
⅓ cup	grated Parmesan cheese	75 mL
3 tablespoons	dried bread crumbs	50 mL

Open oyster shells with an oyster knife; remove oysters and drain well. Wash half the shells and arrange in a shallow pan on rock salt or crumpled foil to keep shells steady. Place oysters in deep end of each shell.

In a saucepan, fry the bacon until crisp and drain well. Return the bacon to the saucepan and melt the butter over moderate heat. Fry the onion and garlic until tender. Add the flour and seasonings and blend well. Pour in the chicken broth and cream and stir until well blended. Cook and stir over moderate heat until sauce is thickened.

Stir a couple of tablespoons of the sauce into the beaten egg yolks and pour egg mixture into saucepan. Bring to a gentle boil and cook, stirring, for a couple of minutes.

Chop the shrimp and add to the sauce with the mushrooms and wine. When sauce is just heated through, remove from heat. Spoon a couple of tablespoons of the mixture over each oyster.

Mix together the Parmesan cheese and bread crumbs; sprinkle over the oysters. Place the pan on the upper grill over medium heat until toasted brown on top.

Cooking Time: 15 minutes

Serves 6 to 8

Calamari (Squid)

A bit of warning with this dish (one of my favourites!). If you serve it with skordalia, don't plan on going out in public — a lot of garlic is used.

4 pounds	small squid, cleaned	2 kg
	Salt	
	Pepper	
	Flour	
	Vegetable oil	
2	lemons, cut into wedges	2

Wash the squid under cold running water and pat dry with paper towel. Cut crosswise into ½-inch (1 cm) thick rings. Sprinkle generously with salt and pepper. Place some flour in a small bowl and add about a dozen of the squid slices, tossing to coat completely.

Heat about 1 inch (2.5 cm) of vegetable oil over high heat in a large skillet. Drop the squid in and cook and turn for a couple of minutes, until golden brown on both sides. Line a platter with paper towel. As the squid are cooked, transfer to platter with a slotted spoon and keep warm while you cook the remainder.

Garnish with lemon wedges and serve with Skordalia (page 178).

Serves 6 to 8

HINT: When draining fried foods, save money by placing pieces of paper towel on top of newspaper. Change the newspaper, not the paper towel.

Frogs' Legs

Store-bought frogs' legs never seem to taste as good as the ones my brother and I used to catch when we were little and bullfrogs were plentiful, but I still enjoy them just as much.

2 pounds	frogs' legs	1 kg
1 cup	dry white wine	250 mL
¼ cup	olive oil	50 mL
3	garlic cloves, crushed	3
1 tablespoon	chopped fresh parsley	15 mL
¼ teaspoon	salt	1 mL
¼ teaspoon	pepper	1 mL

Place the frogs' legs in a shallow pan. Mix together the remaining ingredients and pour over the frogs' legs. Marinate for 2 hours, turning occasionally. Drain and reserve the marinade.

Place the frogs' legs on the upper grill over medium heat, brushing frequently with the reserved marinade and turning halfway through cooking time, until golden brown.

Cooking Time: 15 minutes

Serves 6

Hot Crab Meat Dip

8 oz.	cream cheese, softened	250 g
1 tablespoon	milk	15 mL
1	can crab meat, drained (7 oz./198 g)	1
2 tablespoons	finely minced onion	25 mL
1 teaspoon	horseradish	5 mL
¼ teaspoon	salt	1 mL
Pinch	cayenne pepper	Pinch
½ cup	toasted sliced almonds	125 mL

Mix together all ingredients except the almonds. Spoon into a heatproof dish and sprinkle with the almonds.

Place on upper grill over medium heat. Serve hot with crackers.

Cooking Time: 15 minutes

Serves 6 to 8

Shrimp Coquille

My husband couldn't find my Shrimp Coquille recipe one evening so he made up his own. I never would have thought of putting grated carrot in it! I must admit, I like his version much better than my own.

2 tablespoons	butter	25 mL
2	green onions, finely chopped	2
1	garlic clove, crushed	1
1	medium carrot, grated	1
1 cup	sour cream	250 mL
½ teaspoon	paprika	2 mL
	Salt to taste	
	Pepper to taste	
1 pound	small cooked shrimp	500 g
½ cup	soft buttered bread crumbs	125 mL
½ cup	shredded mozzarella cheese	125 mL

Melt the butter in a large skillet over moderate heat. Add the onion, garlic and carrot; sauté until just tender. Add the sour cream, seasonings and shrimp; cook until heated through.

Spoon mixture into 8 coquille shells and top with buttered bread crumbs. Top with cheese.

Place on upper grill over medium-high heat, watching carefully as it will burn easily.

Cooking Time: 5 minutes

Serves 8

Escargots à la Bourguignonne

I much prefer this recipe using the mushroom caps. You can eat the container and eliminate the difficult job of washing the escargot shells.

1	can escargots, drained (5 oz./125 g)	1
24	escargot shells or 16 large mushroom caps	24
4 tablespoons	butter	50 mL
1 teaspoon	minced garlic	5 mL
1 tablespoon	chopped fresh parsley	15 mL
	French bread	

Place escargots in shells or mushroom caps. You will be able to fit more than one in the larger mushroom caps.

In a small bowl, blend together the butter, minced garlic and parsley. (You may prefer to use more garlic.) Stuff butter mixture into shells or spread on mushroom caps.

Place in escargot dishes or on a foil plate. Place on upper grill over high heat until everything is sizzling. Serve immediately with chunks of French bread to soak up the garlic butter.

Cooking Time: 10 minutes

Serves 4

Rumaki

½ cup	soya sauce	125 mL
1 tablespoon	sugar	15 mL
1	can water chestnuts, drained	1
	(10 oz./284 mL)	
	Sliced raw bacon	

In a small deep bowl, mix together the soya sauce and sugar until the sugar is dissolved. Add water chestnuts to the mixture, tossing to coat completely. Marinate for a couple of hours, stirring frequently.

Roll each water chestnut in a slice of bacon. Fasten with a tooth-pick.

Preheat barbecue on high and turn to low 2 or 3 minutes before adding rumaki. Place on lower grill on a sheet of perforated foil (to prevent flare-ups), turning frequently until bacon is cooked. (You may also cook rumaki on a griddle for a slightly longer time.) Serve hot.

Cooking Time: 8 minutes

Serves 4 to 6

Pesto Mushrooms

1 pound	mushrooms	500 g
	Pesto Sauce (page 173)	
	Swiss cheese	

Remove the stems from the mushroom caps and wipe the caps clean. Place caps on fish grill or griddle (off the barbecue). Spoon Pesto Sauce into each mushroom cap and top with a bit of shredded or sliced Swiss cheese.

Place on the upper grill over medium heat until the cheese has melted.

Cooking Time: 10 minutes

Serves 4 to 6

HINT: The best way to store fresh mushrooms is in a paper bag, not plastic, in the refrigerator. Do not clean mushrooms until just before using. Do not soak or scrub; just wipe with a damp cloth and dry with paper towel.

Artichoke Squares

1	can artichoke hearts (14 oz./398 mL)	1
¼ cup	olive oil	50 mL
1	small onion, finely chopped	1
4	eggs	4
2 cups	shredded mozzarella cheese	500 mL
⅓ cup	dried bread crumbs	75 mL
2 tablespoons	chopped fresh parsley	25 mL
½ teaspoon	salt	2 mL
¼ teaspoon	pepper	1 mL

Drain the artichokes and chop finely. Set aside. In a small saucepan, cook the onion in the oil over moderate heat until it is tender.

In a medium bowl, beat the eggs until well blended. Add the cooked onions, chopped artichoke, mozzarella cheese, bread crumbs and seasonings.

Grease a 12-inch by 8-inch (3.5 L) pan and spread the mixture in evenly.

Place on upper grill over medium-low heat until mixture is set and lightly browned. Let cool slightly before cutting into serving pieces.

Cooking Time: 30 minutes

Serves 8

Spinach Squares

1	package frozen chopped spinach (10 oz./284 g)	1
1 cup	flour	250 mL
1 cup	milk	250 mL
2	eggs	2
½ teaspoon	salt	2 mL
¼ teaspoon	pepper	1 mL
1 pound	Cheddar cheese, shredded	500 g
1	medium onion, finely chopped	1

Boil and drain spinach. Set aside. Mix together remaining ingredients. Mix in spinach. Press into 9-inch square (2.5 L) pan.

Place on upper grill over medium-low heat until mixture is set. Let cool slightly before cutting into serving pieces.

Cooking Time: 30 minutes

Serves 8

Baked Brie

2-pound	wheel of Brie	1 kg
⅓ cup	chopped fresh parsley	75 mL
⅓ cup	sun-dried tomatoes	75 mL
8 sheets	phyllo pastry	8
¼ cup	butter, melted	50 mL

Cut the Brie in half horizontally. Sprinkle the bottom half with the chopped parsley. Boil the dried tomatoes in water for 2 minutes and drain. Chop them and sprinkle on the parsley. Replace the top half of the Brie and set aside.

Lay out one sheet of phyllo, 17 inches by 12 inches (42 cm by 30 cm), and brush with melted butter. Place Brie in centre of phyllo and wrap, pressing phyllo against cheese. Lay out another sheet of phyllo and brush with melted butter. Turn Brie over and place in centre of sheet. Wrap as before. Do this twice more, turning the Brie each time.

Lay out four more sheets of phyllo on top of one another, brushing each with butter. Place Brie in centre and fold sides up to cover completely and bunch up in centre, twisting a bit. Gently brush with remaining butter and place in a greased pan.

Place on upper grill of barbecue over medium-low heat until phyllo is golden brown.

Cooking Time: 15 minutes

Place baked Brie in refrigerator for about 1 hour or until it is room temperature. If served hot, the cheese will be too soft and runny.

Serves about 24

Phyllo pastry is a thin paper-like dough that makes a flaky crust. It is traditionally Greek and may be bought fresh or frozen.

Bruschetta

Bruschetta is wonderful as an appetizer or as an accompaniment to almost any meal. You may also sprinkle on top 1 cup (250 mL) shredded mozzarella cheese before heating.

1	loaf crusty Italian bread	1
¼ cup	virgin olive oil	50 mL
1 tablespoon	chopped fresh parsley	15 mL
4	garlic cloves, crushed	4
4	sun-dried tomatoes, chopped finely	4
	or	
3	medium tomatoes, chopped	3

Cut the bread in half horizontally and lay out flat. Mix together the remaining ingredients and spoon over the bread.

Place on the upper grill over low heat until golden, being careful not to burn. Slice into individual portions and serve warm.

Cooking Time: 3 minutes

Serves 4

Nachos

Keep these ingredients on hand — you can feed a whole crew with very little fuss.

Spread tortilla chips on a foil-covered pan. Spoon Antipasta (page 38) or Salsa (page 175) over top of chips. If you like it hot, top with some jalapeño chilies cut into small pieces or strips. Sprinkle with lots of shredded Cheddar or Monterey Jack cheese.

Place on upper grill over low heat until heated through and cheese has melted. Serve immediately.

Antipasta

This is wonderful as an appetizer served with crackers.

3	cans tuna with oil, undrained (each 6½ oz./184 g)	3
6	green peppers, finely chopped	6
1	jar Manzanilla olives, drained and finely chopped (13 oz./375 mL)	1
1	jar small gherkins, drained and finely sliced (13 oz./375 mL)	1
40 oz.	tomato sauce	1.25 mL
1½	bottles chili sauce (each 10 oz./284 mL)	1½
2	cans sliced mushrooms, drained (each 10 oz./284 mL)	2
1 tablespoon	horseradish	15 mL
	Juice of one lemon	
1 tablespoon	Worcestershire sauce	15 mL
2	garlic cloves, minced	2

Mix everything together in a saucepan and boil, stirring often, for about 5 minutes.

Pour into sterilized jars. Keeps for 4 months in refrigerator.

Makes 12 cups (3 L)

Pizza

With so many teenagers in our home, this recipe is a real staple. Since we live in the country, we can't just order out for a pizza. Now that we've developed our own numerous variations, commercial pizzas never taste as good.

1 cup	warm water (110–115°F/43–46°C)	250 mL
1 tablespoon	sugar	15 mL
1 tablespoon	dry yeast (or 1 package)	15 mL
3½ cups	flour	875 mL
1 teaspoon	salt	5 mL
¼ cup	olive oil	50 mL

In a small bowl, dissolve the sugar in the warm water. Add the yeast and stir in gently. Let stand for about 5 minutes in a warm place until a thin layer of foam covers the surface.

In a large bowl, combine 3 cups (750 mL) of the flour and the salt. Add the yeast and oil. Mix together until you have a soft dough. Turn out on a floured board, dust your hands with flour and knead the dough gently for 10 or 15 minutes. Keep adding flour until the dough is no longer sticky. Continue kneading the dough until it is elastic and shiny.

Shape the dough into a ball and place in an oiled bowl, turning to coat with oil. Cover bowl with plastic wrap and let rise for 1 hour in a warm place, until doubled in size. Punch down the dough and shape into a ball. If you are not using it within 2 hours, place back in oiled bowl, turning to coat again, cover with plastic wrap and refrigerate. Let chilled dough return to room temperature before continuing.

Place the dough on a lightly floured surface and lightly dust the top of the dough with flour. Roll out with a rolling pin until it is ¼ inch (5 mm) thick. Place on pan and form a rim around the outer edge with your fingers.

After you have added Tomato Sauce, garnishes or Spinach Topping, place pizza on upper rack over medium-low heat until crust is golden. Watch carefully as crust will burn easily.

Cooking Time: 10 minutes

TOMATO SAUCE

1	can (14 oz./398 mL) Italian stewed tomatoes	1
1	can (14 oz./398 mL) tomato sauce	1
1	can (5½ oz./156 mL) tomato paste	1
2	garlic cloves, crushed	2
1 teaspoon	salt	5 mL
1 teaspoon	oregano	5 mL

GARNISHES

Sautéed chicken in lots of garlic

Sautéed hot Italian sausage in lots of garlic

Cooked hamburger chunks or small balls

Partially cooked bacon pieces

Artichoke hearts, quartered

Fresh mushroom slices

Tomato slices

Green pepper rings

Pineapple chunks

Black olives

Chopped anchovies

Shredded cheeses
(mozzarella, Monterey Jack, Swiss, mixed together)

SPINACH TOPPING

Enjoy this satisfying pizza topping as a change to the tomato sauce and other garnishes.

1 tablespoon	olive oil	15 mL
2	packages frozen chopped spinach, thawed and drained (each 10 oz./284 g)	2
1	small onion, finely chopped	1
4	garlic cloves, minced	4
	Salt to taste	
	Pepper to taste	
4 cups	shredded mozzarella cheese	1 L
1	can plum tomatoes, drained (28 oz./796 mL)	1
1 teaspoon	dried oregano	5 mL
½ teaspoon	salt	2 mL
¼ teaspoon	pepper	1 mL
½ cup	grated Parmesan cheese	125 mL

Heat the olive oil in a skillet and add the spinach. Add the onion, garlic, salt and pepper. Cook and stir for a couple of minutes. Place 2 cups (500 mL) mozzarella cheese in a medium bowl and stir in the spinach. When it is well blended and the cheese has melted, spread out on prepared pizza dough.

Put the drained tomatoes into a small bowl and crush well with potato masher. Mix in the oregano, salt and pepper. Spread tomato mixture over the spinach mixture.

Sprinkle with remaining 2 cups (500 mL) mozzarella cheese and ½ cup (125 mL) grated Parmesan cheese.

Serves 4 to 6

Slush

This is a refreshing drink on a hot afternoon. I usually make up a batch of Slush at the beginning of each summer and leave it in the freezer. It's handy to be able to scoop out some as you need it.

7 cups	water	1.75 L
1½ cups	sugar	375 mL
1	can frozen orange juice (12½ oz./355 mL)	1
1	can frozen lemonade (12½ oz./355 mL)	1
	Ginger ale or soda water	

Prepare 24 hours in advance.

Mix the water and sugar together in a saucepan and bring to a boil. Stir until the sugar is dissolved and liquid is clear. Remove from heat and let cool slightly. Pour into a large jug or pail. Add the frozen orange juice and lemonade concentrates and mix well.

Place in the freezer for approximately 24 hours, until frozen into slush. Spoon enough into a glass to fill it halfway and top with ginger ale or soda water.

Serves 8

You may also add 26 oz. (780 mL) of L.C.B.O. alcohol with the fruit concentrates.

Verry Berry Punch

1	package frozen strawberries (15 oz./426 g)	1
¾ cup	sugar	175 mL
1	bottle cranberry juice, chilled (40 oz./1.2 L)	1
1	bottle soda water, chilled (26 oz./780 mL)	1

Thaw the strawberries and place in blender with the sugar. Let run on high until the mixture is smooth. Pour into a large punch bowl and stir in remaining ingredients. Add ice and keep cold.

Serves 20

You may also add ½ cup (125 mL) of brandy with the sugar and 26 oz. (780 mL) of sparkling white wine, chilled.

Melon Baby

	Ice cubes	
1 cup	watermelon pieces	250 mL
1 oz.	vodka or rum	25 mL
1 oz.	melon liqueur	25 mL
1 tablespoon	sugar	15 mL

Place ice in blender and process until crushed. Scoop out pieces of watermelon with a spoon, making sure to remove all seeds. Add to blender with vodka or rum, melon liqueur and sugar. Process until well blended. Pour into a glass.

Serves 1

Strawberry Daiquiri

This drink, made without the rum, is a favourite with our children.

	Ice cubes	
1 cup	fresh or frozen strawberries	250 mL
1½ oz.	rum	50 mL
1 tablespoon	sugar	15 mL
½ cup	cream	125 mL

Place ice in blender and process until crushed. Add strawberries and process until smooth. Add remaining ingredients and process until smooth. Pour into glass and garnish with fresh strawberry.

Serves 1

Raspberry Syllabub

1 cup	light cream, chilled	250 mL
1 cup	white wine, chilled	250 mL
1 cup	fresh raspberries	250 mL

Place all ingredients in blender and process until liquid. Serve in chilled glasses over crushed ice.

Serves 4

Eggs and Breakfast Dishes

Eggs Mornay

4	eggs	4
2 tablespoons	butter	25 mL
2 tablespoons	flour	25 mL
1 cup	milk	250 mL
¼ pound	shredded Cheddar cheese	125 g
	Salt	
	Pepper	

Hard boil the eggs; cool and peel. Set aside.

Prepare cheese sauce by melting the butter in a medium saucepan over moderate heat. Blend in the flour and slowly add the milk, stirring constantly until thickened. Mix in most of the cheese, reserving a couple of tablespoons (25 mL) to sprinkle on top. Add salt and pepper to taste. Remove from heat.

Cut hard-boiled eggs in half and arrange in a heatproof dish, cut side up. Top with the cheese sauce and sprinkle the reserved cheese on top.

Place on upper grill over medium heat until bubbly on top.

Cooking Time: 20 minutes

Serves 4

EGGS FLORENTINE

Prepare the same as Eggs Mornay, but place the eggs on a bed of cooked spinach, then cover with the cheese sauce.

EGGS AU GRATIN

Prepare the same as Eggs Mornay, but top the cheese sauce with a layer of dried bread crumbs and then the shredded cheese.

HINT: When frying eggs, break the eggs into shaped cookie cutters to make your children's breakfast more interesting.

Bacon & Eggs
in Muffin Tins

This works great when you have a lot of people to feed for breakfast. You can prepare the right amount for each person with no leftovers and no one going hungry.

Press a wide strip of bacon around the inside wall of each cup of your muffin tin. Break an egg into each cup and sprinkle with salt and pepper and perhaps a bit of paprika or some chopped chives.

Place on upper grill over medium-low heat until eggs are done as you like them.

Cooking Time: 10 to 15 minutes

Green Eggs & Ham

If your children are familiar with Dr. Seuss, they'll love this dish! Of course, when I serve it to adults, they usually end up talking about their favourite books and characters when they were children.

6	eggs	6
4	green onions	4
3 tablespoons	cream	50 mL
3 tablespoons	chopped fresh parsley	50 mL
½ teaspoon	salt	2 mL
	Fresh ground pepper	
1 cup	diced cooked ham	250 mL
2 tablespoons	butter	25 mL

In a medium bowl, beat the eggs with a wire whisk. Chop the green onions, including 2 inches (5 cm) of the green tops, and add to the eggs. Add the remaining ingredients, except the butter, and stir well.

Place the griddle on the lower grill and preheat on medium-low for 5 to 10 minutes. (This is so the eggs will begin to cook immediately and not flow out of control.) Grease the griddle with the butter. Pour the egg mixture on the griddle and cook, scrambling, until light and fluffy.

Cooking Time: 5 minutes

Serves 4

Eggs Baked
in Potato Skins

4	large baked potatoes	4
8	eggs	8
	Salt	
	Pepper	
	Chopped chives	
3 tablespoons	butter	50 mL
2 tablespoons	chopped onion	25 mL
1 tablespoon	chopped chives	15 mL

Slice the baked potatoes in half lengthwise and remove three-quarters of the pulp to a bowl, being careful not to damage the skins.

Break the eggs into the halved potato skins and sprinkle with salt, pepper and chopped chives.

Mash the pulp with the butter, onion, 1 tablespoon (15 mL) chopped chives and salt and pepper to taste.

Preheat a large skillet or griddle over high heat. Reduce heat to medium-high and oil the griddle well. Spoon on the mashed potato and flatten with a spatula. Place baked potatoes with eggs on grill.

Turn potato cake when golden brown on bottom and brown other side. Bake the potato skins until the egg whites are set.

Cooking Time: 10 minutes

Serves 8

HINT: To speed up cooking time for baked potatoes, run metal skewers through them. The skewers help heat up the inside of the potato.

Pancakes

1 cup	flour	250 mL
½ teaspoon	salt	2 mL
1 teaspoon	baking powder	5 mL
2 tablespoons	sugar	25 mL
1	egg	1
1 cup	milk	250 mL
2 tablespoons	melted butter	25 mL

Mix together the dry ingredients. Beat the egg well and mix together with the milk and melted butter. Blend into the dry ingredients until just moistened, letting some of the lumps remain.

Grease griddle with a little vegetable oil and place on the upper grill to preheat for 5 to 10 minutes on high. Pour the pancake batter onto the griddle and cook with lid down, turning once, until golden.

Cooking Time: 3 or 4 minutes on each side

Serves 4

VARIATIONS

BLUEBERRY PANCAKES: Add ½ cup (125 mL) fresh blueberries

APPLE PANCAKES: Add ½ cup (125 mL) finely chopped apples

BUTTERMILK PANCAKES: Use buttermilk in place of milk

SAUCES

When we run out of maple syrup, or for a bit of a change, we use different sauces. If I have the time I make my own or sometimes use canned blueberry or cherry pie filling. Just heat in a small pot on the barbecue and serve on the side.

BLUEBERRY GLAZE

1 cup	sugar	250 mL
2 tablespoons	cornstarch	25 mL
1 cup	water	250 mL
½ cup	fresh blueberries	125 mL

Mix together the sugar and cornstarch in a small pot. Gradually stir in water until well blended. Crush blueberries and add to the mixture. Cook over moderate heat until mixture boils and continue to boil for a couple of minutes until thick and clear.

HINT: Add various fruits to pancakes for a more exotic breakfast. Try kiwi, mango or pineapple.

Seasoned Hash Browns

4	large potatoes	4
2	green onions, chopped	2
½ teaspoon	salt	2 mL
	Fresh ground pepper	
1½ teaspoons	paprika	7 mL
Pinch	garlic salt	Pinch
1 tablespoon	toasted sesame seeds (optional)	15 mL
3 tablespoons	melted butter	50 mL

OR

Frozen hash browns
(¾ to 1 cup/175 to 250 mL per person)

Chopped chives

Salt to taste

Pepper to taste

1 tablespoon (15 mL) butter
per cup (250 mL) hash browns

Scrub the potatoes and dice finely. Place in a medium bowl and toss with the green onions, seasonings and sesame seeds. Lay the mixture on a double-thickness of foil or a single-thickness of heavy-duty foil, 18 inches by 12 inches (46 cm by 30 cm). Sprinkle with the melted butter and seal securely.

Place on the upper grill over medium heat until fork-tender.

OR

Grease a 12-inch by 10-inch (30 cm by 25 cm) pan with vegetable oil. Spread out the hash browns and sprinkle with seasonings. Toss slightly. Drizzle with melted butter.

Place on lower grill over medium heat, tossing occasionally.

Cooking Time: 20 minutes

Beef
and
Pork

Sesame Sirloin

This is my all-time favourite way to cook steak. You can serve everyone steak done to their liking and there is no waste — the strips are great heated up for breakfast.

½ cup	vegetable oil	125 mL
¼ cup	sesame seeds	50 mL
½ cup	soya sauce	125 mL
¼ cup	lemon juice	50 mL
2 teaspoons	sugar	10 mL
¼ teaspoon	pepper	1 mL
2	garlic cloves, crushed	2
2	medium onions, sliced, in rings	2
4 pounds	beef top sirloin steak, 2 inches (5 cm) thick	2 kg

In a small skillet, mix together the oil and sesame seeds. Cook over moderate heat, stirring constantly, until the sesame seeds are toasted. Remove from heat and mix together with the soya sauce, lemon juice, sugar, pepper, garlic and onion rings.

Pour into a shallow pan and add the meat, turning to coat completely. Refrigerate for 3 or 4 hours, turning steak occasionally. Remove steak from pan, reserving the marinade.

Barbecue on the lower grill over medium heat, basting occasionally with the reserved marinade.

Cooking Time: 15 minutes on each side

This cooking method will provide you with rare steak in the centre, medium on the outside. For well-done steak, increase your cooking time by approximately 5 minutes.

To serve, place steak on a large platter and cut into strips. Your guests may then choose according to their preference.

Serves 4 to 6

Blackened Steak

Blackened Seasoning may also be used on seafood and chicken breasts.

| 4 | rib eye filets, 1 inch (2.5 cm) thick | 4 |

BLACKENED SEASONING

¼ teaspoon	salt	1 mL
½ teaspoon	black pepper	2 mL
½ teaspoon	white pepper	2 mL
¼ teaspoon	cayenne pepper (use ½ teaspoon/2 mL if you like it really hot!)	1 mL
½ teaspoon	garlic powder	2 mL
½ teaspoon	onion powder	2 mL
½ teaspoon	crushed dried thyme	2 mL
1 tablespoon	melted butter	15 mL

Mix together the Blackened Seasoning ingredients. Blend with the melted butter.

Brush all over one side of the steaks. If you like it really hot, you can brush it on both sides.

Place steaks on the lower grill over high heat for rare steaks; use a lower temperature for medium to well-done steaks. Turn only once, using tongs.

Cooking Time: 5 minutes for each side for medium

Serves 4

Grilled Roast Beef

4-pound	beef tenderloin or blade roast	2 kg
	Olive oil	
	Fresh ground pepper	
	Garlic salt	

Insert the spit rod through the centre of the roast of beef or place in a foil pan. Rub all over with the olive oil and sprinkle liberally with pepper and garlic salt.

Preheat the barbecue on high for about 10 minutes. Place the roast on the upper grill, over high heat, for 5 minutes to sear. Move over to unheated lower grill, reduce heat to medium, and continue cooking with indirect heat.

If using rotisserie, place over high indirect heat for 5 minutes. Reduce heat to medium and continue cooking.

Cooking Time: 15 minutes per pound for medium-rare

Insert meat thermometer in centre of meat, being careful not to let it touch the spit if using rotisserie.

Rare	140°F (60°C)
Medium	160°F (70°C)
Well-done	170°F (80°C)

Serves 6 to 8

Beef Teriyaki

2-pound	beef round steak, 1 inch (2.5 cm) thick	1 kg
½ cup	soya sauce	125 mL
½ cup	dry sherry	125 mL
1 tablespoon	sesame oil	15 mL
¼ cup	brown sugar	50 mL
2	garlic cloves, crushed	2
1 tablespoon	fresh ginger, minced	15 mL
1	small pineapple, cut into 1-inch (2.5 cm) pieces	1

Cut the steak into strips ¼ inch (5 mm) wide and 3 inches (8 cm) long.

Mix together the remaining ingredients, except the pineapple, in a medium bowl. Add the meat and toss to coat well. Marinate for 2 hours, tossing occasionally. Drain, reserving the marinade.

Thread the beef on metal skewers, accordion-style, alternately with the pineapple chunks. Skewer the meat loosely and do so just before cooking, as the pineapple tenderizes the meat very quickly and will turn it mushy.

Place on the lower grill over medium heat, turning and basting with the reserved marinade.

Cooking Time: 10 minutes

Serves 6

Texas Ribs

4 pounds	meaty short ribs of beef	2 kg
1 tablespoon	vegetable oil	15 mL
1 tablespoon	cider vinegar	15 mL
¼ cup	soya sauce	50 mL
Dash	hot pepper sauce	Dash
1	garlic clove, crushed	1
1 tablespoon	brown sugar	15 mL
½ teaspoon	dry mustard	2 mL
¼ teaspoon	cayenne pepper	1 mL

Place the ribs in a large pot and cover with water. Bring to a boil and simmer for about 30 minutes, until fork-tender. Drain well. Place in a shallow pan.

Prepare the marinade by mixing together the remaining ingredients. Pour over the ribs, turning to coat completely. Marinate for 2 hours, turning occasionally. Drain, reserving the marinade.

Place the ribs on the upper grill over medium-low heat, turning and basting frequently with the reserved marinade.

Cooking Time: 20 minutes

Serves 4

Hot pepper sauce, such as Tabasco sauce, is made from chili peppers and can be very hot. Use only a few drops to season sauces.

Mexicali Burgers

We are always looking for ways to make our burgers more interesting. This one is a real favourite.

1½ pounds	ground beef	750 g
2	eggs, lightly beaten	2
1	small onion, minced	1
1	garlic clove, minced	1
1	jalapeño chili, minced	1
1 teaspoon	chili powder	5 mL
½ teaspoon	cumin	2 mL
1 teaspoon	salt	5 mL
1 cup	tomato salsa (commercial or the Salsa recipe on page 175)	250 mL
½ cup	shredded Cheddar cheese	125 mL
1½ cups	dried bread crumbs or crushed tortilla chips	375 mL

Mix together all the ingredients until well blended. Divide the mixture evenly and shape into patties.

Place on the upper grill over medium heat, turning halfway through cooking time.

Serve on buttered toasted buns. Heat the buns on the upper rack while cooking the second side of the burgers.

Cooking Time: 7 minutes on each side

Serves 6 to 8

Feta Burgers

1½ pounds	ground beef or lamb	750 g
2	eggs, lightly beaten	2
1	small onion, minced	1
1	garlic clove, minced	1
1 teaspoon	salt	5 mL
¼ teaspoon	pepper	1 mL
1 teaspoon	dried dill	5 mL
½ cup	crumbled feta cheese	125 mL
¾ to 1 cup	dried bread crumbs	175 to 250 mL

Mix all ingredients together until well blended. Divide the mixture evenly and shape into patties.

Place on upper grill over medium heat, turning halfway through cooking time.

Serve on buttered toasted buns. Heat the buns on the upper rack while cooking the second side of the burgers.

Cooking Time: 7 minutes on each side

Serves 6 to 8

Sweet Mustard Pork Chops

6	large ¾-inch (2 cm) thick pork chops	6
½	bottle beer	½
1 tablespoon	honey mustard	15 mL
	Fresh ground pepper	
1 teaspoon	dried tarragon	5 mL
2 tablespoons	melted butter	25 mL

Lay out the pork chops on a platter. In a small microwave-safe bowl, blend together remaining ingredients. Microwave for about 30 seconds to heat through and remelt the butter. Brush liberally on both sides of pork chops. Marinate for 2 hours.

Baste again and place on the upper grill over high heat until browned. Baste again, turn and reduce heat to medium.

Cooking Time: 8 minutes for each side

Serves 6

Smoky Southern Ribs

I experimented for years to come up with a recipe for ribs that tasted like those in the South. When travelling I often asked rib-house owners for their recipes, but they are all a well-kept secret. I think this recipe just about fits the bill.

1 cup	tomato sauce	250 mL
½ cup	chili sauce	125 mL
¼ cup	cider vinegar	50 mL
2 tablespoons	Worcestershire sauce	25 mL
3 tablespoons	Liquid Smoke	50 mL
1 tablespoon	molasses	15 mL
¼ teaspoon	hot pepper sauce	1 mL
¼ cup	brown sugar	50 mL
1	medium onion, chopped	1
½	lemon, sliced	½
1 teaspoon	dry mustard	5 mL
¼ teaspoon	cayenne pepper	1 mL
1 teaspoon	salt	5 mL
¼ teaspoon	pepper	1 mL
3 to 4 pounds	pork spareribs	1.5 to 2 kg

Mix all of the ingredients, except the spareribs, in a medium saucepan. Bring to a boil, reduce heat and simmer for 20 minutes.

Place ribs in a large saucepan and cover with water. Bring to a boil and simmer for about 30 minutes, until fork-tender. Drain well.

Place ribs on upper grill over low heat, basting with the sauce and turning frequently so they will not dry out and burn. Meat will pull away from the ends of the bones when it is done.

If you don't have time to parboil the ribs, use low heat and long, slow grilling time to ensure they are well done without burning on the outside.

Cooking Time: 20 minutes

Serves 4

Liquid Smoke is a mixture of water and natural liquid smoke. It adds extra barbecue flavour and can be used directly on meat or in sauces.

Pork Tenderloin with Mango Sauce

The Mango Sauce is a wonderful combination with pork tenderloin and will have everyone asking what's in it.

2	pork tenderloins, total weight 2 pounds (1 kg)	2
	Vegetable oil	
1 teaspoon	thyme	5 mL
1 teaspoon	tarragon	5 mL
½ teaspoon	pepper	2 mL

MANGO SAUCE

1	mango, puréed	1
2 tablespoons	lemon juice	25 mL
2 tablespoons	sugar	25 mL
1 teaspoon	minced fresh ginger	5 mL

Rub the pork tenderloins all over with a bit of vegetable oil. Combine the thyme, tarragon and pepper; sprinkle mixture over the meat.

Preheat the barbecue for 10 minutes. Place the tenderloins on the upper grill over high heat for 5 (summer) to 10 (winter) minutes to sear. Turn meat and reduce heat to medium. Cook until meat thermometer registers 160°F (70°C).

Cooking Time: 20 minutes

While meat is cooking, prepare Mango Sauce. Combine all sauce ingredients in a small saucepan and heat over low heat, stirring, until sugar is dissolved. Keep warm.

Let meat stand for 5 minutes before carving. Slice into ¼-inch (5 mm) slices and spoon a little Mango Sauce over top when serving.

Serves 6

Mango is a sturdy yellow fruit, somewhat like a peach but with firmer skin. Ripe mangoes have yellow to red smooth skin that yields to gentle pressure. Peel the skin from the stem end.

Asian Pork Kabobs

2 pounds	lean pork shoulder or loin	1 kg
¼ cup	olive oil	50 mL
¼ cup	lime or lemon juice	50 mL
2	garlic cloves, crushed	2
1 tablespoon	chopped parsley or cilantro	15 mL
2 teaspoons	chopped lemon grass	10 mL
	or green onion	

Cut the pork into 1-inch (2.5 cm) cubes.

Mix together the remaining ingredients in a large bowl. Add the pork and toss to coat completely. Cover and refrigerate for 2 hours. Drain, reserving the marinade.

Thread the meat onto 6 long metal skewers, ¼ inch (5 mm) apart to ensure complete cooking all the way through.

Place on the lower grill over medium heat, with the lid down, turning and basting occasionally with the reserved marinade.

Cooking Time: 20 minutes

Serves 6

Stuffed Pork Loin Roast with Clove-Orange Baste

4- to 5-pound	loin of pork, boned	2 to 2.2 kg

STUFFING

2 tablespoons	butter	25 mL
2 tablespoons	minced onion	25 mL
½ pound	fresh mushrooms, chopped	250 g
¼ cup	chopped fresh basil	50 mL
¼ teaspoon	salt	1 mL
¼ teaspoon	pepper	1 mL
1 cup	soft bread crumbs	250 mL

BASTE

¾ cup	frozen orange juice concentrate, thawed	175 mL
2 tablespoons	brown sugar	25 mL
¼ teaspoon	ground cloves	1 mL

Melt the butter in a skillet and add the onions and chopped mushrooms. Cook very briefly, until just tender. Remove to a bowl and add the remaining stuffing ingredients, blending well.

Unroll the pork loin and lay out flat. Spoon the stuffing over the meat, roll up and tie every 2 or 3 inches (5 or 8 cm) with string.

Mix together the basting ingredients.

Place meat on the upper grill over medium-low heat until meat thermometer registers 185°F (85°C) and meat is no longer pink. Baste for the last hour of cooking time.

Cooking Time: 3 hours

Serves 6 to 8

Maple Ham Steak

This is a great way to take advantage of our wonderful Canadian maple syrup.

2-pound	ham steak, 1 inch (2.5 cm) thick	1 kg
¼ cup	vegetable oil	50 mL
¼ cup	lime juice	50 mL
¼ cup	maple syrup	50 mL
2 teaspoons	honey mustard	10 mL
1 teaspoon	grated fresh ginger	5 mL

Slash the edges of the ham to prevent curling. Place in a shallow pan.

Mix together the remaining ingredients. Pour over the ham steak, turning to coat completely. Marinate for 2 hours.

Place ham on the upper grill over medium heat, brushing with reserved marinade occasionally. Turn once. When completely cooked, remove to a serving platter and pour marinade over top.

Cooking Time: 8 minutes on each side

Serves 4

Fruit-Glazed Ham with Cloves

4-pound	cooked boneless ham	2 kg
	Whole cloves	

ORANGE-APRICOT GLAZE

¼ cup	orange marmalade or apricot preserves	50 mL
1 tablespoon	soya sauce	15 mL
2 teaspoons	honey mustard	10 mL

OR

APPLE GLAZE

¼ cup	apple jelly	50 mL
1 tablespoon	apple juice	15 mL
2 teaspoons	honey mustard	10 mL

Score the fat surface of the ham in diamond shapes. Insert cloves in the cross-sections of the diamonds.

Place the ham on the rotisserie, securing tightly with holding forks and balancing carefully. Cook over low heat (300°F/150°C) with the lid down. If you have a two-burner barbecue, turn heat on the other side, using indirect heat.

Meanwhile, prepare one of the glazes. Mix the ingredients together in a small saucepan over low heat. Apply the glaze to the ham for the last 20 minutes of cooking.

Cooking Time: 1½ to 2 hours

Serves 8

Kids' Menu

You can make a children's party a lot more interesting if you offer them a variety of hot dogs. Post a menu (for those who can read) to save yourself from having to answer a million questions.

WHISTLE DOG

Garnish with Cheddar cheese and bacon

CONEY ISLAND DOG

Garnish with Cheddar cheese, chili sauce and hot peppers

TEX MEX DOG

Garnish with melted Monterey Jack cheese, salsa and sour cream

BBQ DOG

Garnish with BBQ sauce and bacon

YODEL DOG

Garnish with Swiss cheese

CAJUN DOG

Garnish with Cajun sauce, salsa and Monterey Jack cheese

Lamb
and
Poultry

Kibbi

Kibbi is traditionally Lebanese or Syrian. A bit of extra work but
well worth the effort.

STUFFING

2 tablespoons	olive oil	25 mL
⅓ cup	pine nuts	75 mL
¼ cup	finely chopped onions	50 mL
½ pound	ground lamb	250 g
½ teaspoon	salt	2 mL
¼ teaspoon	allspice	1 mL
¼ teaspoon	pepper	1 mL

PATTIES

1 cup	bulghur	250 mL
2 pounds	ground lamb	1 kg
¼ cup	minced onion	50 mL
¼ teaspoon	nutmeg	1 mL
Pinch	cayenne pepper	Pinch
1½ teaspoons	salt	7 mL
¼ teaspoon	pepper	1 mL

Prepare the stuffing: In a heavy skillet, heat the olive oil over
moderate heat. Add the pine nuts, brown lightly, and transfer to a
plate with a slotted spoon. Add the onions to the skillet and stir
and cook until soft and transparent. Add the lamb and mash with
the back of a spoon. Cook until there is no trace of pink. Drain off
excess fat and add the seasonings and toasted pine nuts. Set aside.

Prepare the patties: Place the bulghur in a bowl and cover with cold water. Let soak for about 15 minutes, then drain well in a colander lined with cheesecloth and squeeze dry. Mix the bulghur with the remaining patty ingredients. Blend well.

Divide the patty mixture into 8 portions and roll them into patties about 4 inches (10 cm) long and 3 inches (8 cm) wide. Make a well in the centre of each patty with your fingers. Fill with the stuffing, pressing it in well. Bring the sides of the patty up around the stuffing, enclosing it completely and sealing the patty.

Place patties on lower grill over high heat.

Cooking Time: Cook for 10 minutes, turn and cook for another 10 minutes

Serves 6 to 8

Lamb Burgers

For a lamb cheese burger, top with crumbled feta cheese.

1½ pounds	ground lamb	750 g
2	eggs, lightly beaten	2
2 tablespoons	tahini	25 mL
1 tablespoon	chopped parsley	15 mL
1 tablespoon	chopped cilantro	15 mL
1 teaspoon	salt	5 mL
¼ teaspoon	pepper	1 mL
½ cup	grated Parmesan cheese	125 mL
¾ to 1 cup	dried bread crumbs	175 to 250 mL

Mix together all the ingredients until well blended. Divide the mixture evenly and shape into patties.

Place on the upper grill over medium heat, turning halfway through cooking time.

Serve on buttered toasted buns. Heat the buns on the upper rack while cooking second side of burgers.

Cooking Time: 7 minutes on each side

Serves 6 to 8

Tahini is a paste made from ground sesame seeds. It is used in Middle Eastern cooking and is available in specialty food stores.

Souvlaki

Be sure never to marinate Souvlaki overnight. The lamb will absorb too much of the salt, greatly affecting the taste of the meat.

2 pounds	lean lamb, in 2-inch (5 cm) cubes	1 kg
1	large onion, sliced, in rings	1
2 tablespoons	olive oil	25 mL
¼ cup	lemon juice	50 mL
½ teaspoon	salt	2 mL
½ teaspoon	fresh ground pepper	2 mL
2 tablespoons	whipping cream	25 mL

Drop the onion rings into a deep bowl, sprinkle with olive oil, lemon juice, salt and pepper. Add the lamb, tossing to coat well. Marinate at room temperature for 2 hours, tossing occasionally.

Thread lamb tightly on long metal skewers. Brush the meat evenly on all sides with the cream.

Place on the lower grill over medium heat, with the lid down, turning frequently.

Cooking Time: 15 to 20 minutes

Serves 6

Lamb Marinated in Red Wine and Herbs

8	lamb chops,	8
	cut 1 inch (2.5 cm) thick	
½ cup	dry red wine	125 mL
1 tablespoon	olive oil	15 mL
2	garlic cloves, minced	2
1 teaspoon	dried mint	5 mL
½ teaspoon	dried rosemary	2 mL

Mix together the marinating ingredients. Marinate chops for 1 hour. Place lamb chops on lower grill over medium heat, turning halfway through cooking time.

Cooking Time: 10 minutes on each side

Serves 4

Leg of Lamb
Seasoned with Herbs

We raise sheep on our farm and love leg of lamb so much that we joke about trying to raise animals with eight legs.

1 cup	dry red wine	250 mL
3 tablespoons	olive oil	50 mL
1 teaspoon	dried rosemary	5 mL
½ teaspoon	garlic powder	2 mL
½ teaspoon	dried oregano	2 mL
¼ teaspoon	pepper	1 mL
4- to 5-pound	leg of lamb	2 to 2.2 kg

In a small bowl, mix together the wine, olive oil and seasonings.

Remove fell (the paper-like pink layer) from the surface of the meat. Trim any excess fat. Place lamb in a shallow pan and pour over the prepared mixture. Cover and marinate for 4 hours or overnight in refrigerator.

Preheat barbecue on high for about 10 minutes. Sear the leg of lamb on the upper grill over high heat for 5 to 10 minutes. Move over to unheated lower grill, reduce heat to medium, and continue cooking with indirect heat. You may also use the rotisserie over medium indirect heat. Use meat thermometer to test for doneness (170°F/80°C for medium and 180°F/85°C for well-done).

Let rest for 10 minutes before carving.

Cooking Time: Approximately 2 hours

Serves 6 to 8

Lamb Roast Stuffed with Indian Rice

4- to 5-pound	shoulder roast of lamb, boned	2 to 2.2 kg
	Olive oil	
1 cup	water	250 mL
Pinch	saffron threads	Pinch
½ cup	long-grain rice	125 mL
1 tablespoon	thinly sliced lemon grass (or 4 green onions, chopped)	15 mL
¼ cup	chopped fresh parsley	50 mL
2	garlic cloves, finely chopped	2
¼ cup	toasted pine nuts	50 mL
½ teaspoon	salt	2 mL
¼ teaspoon	pepper	1 mL

Bring the water and saffron threads to a boil; add the rice. Cover and cook until tender and water is absorbed. Cool to room temperature.

Combine the cooked rice with the remaining ingredients and blend well. Lay the lamb out flat with the outside down. Spread the rice mixture down the centre of the meat. Fold over the two sides of the lamb and tie every few inches with wet string. Rub the lamb all over with a bit of oil.

Place on the upper grill over medium-low heat, turning halfway through the cooking time.

Let rest for 5 or 10 minutes before carving.

Cooking Time: 1½ hours

Serves 6 to 8

Seasoned Lamb Roast

4- to 5-pound	shoulder roast or leg of lamb	2 to 2.2 kg
	Juice of half a lemon	
½ teaspoon	salt	2 mL
½ teaspoon	garlic powder	2 mL
½ teaspoon	crushed peppercorns	2 mL
½ teaspoon	paprika	2 mL

Rub the roast all over with the lemon juice. Mix together the seasonings in a small bowl and sprinkle over the meat.

Place on the upper grill over high heat to sear. Move over to unheated lower grill, reduce heat to medium, and continue cooking with indirect heat. You may also use the rotisserie over medium indirect heat. Smoke with wood chips for added flavour. (We like to use apple.)

Let rest 10 minutes before carving.

Cooking Time: Approximately 2 hours

Medium	170°F (80°C)	
Well-done	180°F (85°C)	

Serves 6 to 8

This mixture of seasoning may also be used on beef, pork and chicken.

Tandoori Chicken

1	whole chicken, cut up (or chicken breasts)	1

MARINADE

1	small onion, chopped	1
3	garlic cloves, chopped	3
1 tablespoon	coarsely chopped fresh ginger	15 mL
2 tablespoons	lemon juice	25 mL
½ teaspoon	garam masala	2 mL
½ teaspoon	ground cumin	2 mL
½ teaspoon	turmeric	2 mL
½ teaspoon	salt	2 mL
¼ teaspoon	cayenne pepper	1 mL
1 cup	plain yogourt	250 mL

Place all of the marinade ingredients, except the yogourt, in a blender and process until smooth. Stir in the yogourt.

Remove the skin from the chicken and cut deep slits in the chicken pieces at 1-inch (2.5 cm) intervals. Place in a dish and pour the marinade over the chicken, turning to coat completely. Rub the marinade into the chicken and work it into the slits. Marinate for 4 hours in refrigerator, turning occasionally. Remove the chicken, reserving the marinade.

Place chicken pieces on the upper grill over medium heat, basting with the reserved marinade.

Cooking Time: 8 minutes on each side

Serves 4

Garam masala is a combination of ground spices including carda-mom, cinnamon, cloves, coriander, cumin and nutmeg. It is used in Indian cooking and is available on spice racks in specialty food stores.

HINT: To crush seeds such as cumin, caraway, cardamom and mustard, place a few whole seeds in between two spoons. Grind spoons together, continuing until you have the consistency you need.

Rack of Lamb with Mint-Orange Baste

2	racks of lamb, 1½ to 2 pounds (750 g to 1 kg) each, trimmed	2
2	garlic cloves, crushed	2

MINT-ORANGE BASTE

½ cup	orange juice	125 mL
1 tablespoon	vegetable oil	15 mL
2 tablespoons	brown sugar	25 mL
½ teaspoon	dried mint	2 mL

Rub racks of lamb all over with the crushed garlic. Wrap foil around the bone tips to prevent them from charring and breaking.

Mix all the baste ingredients together in a small saucepan. Cook over low heat, stirring to dissolve the sugar. Keep warm.

Place the lamb on the upper grill over low heat, turning halfway through the cooking time. Brush frequently with the baste.

Cooking Time: 1 hour

Serves 4

Yogourt Chicken

This is possibly the most tender chicken you will ever eat. The yogourt is the secret ingredient that makes it so succulent.

½ cup	plain yogourt	125 mL
1	green onion, chopped	1
1 teaspoon	crushed oregano	5 mL
1 teaspoon	salt	5 mL
¼ teaspoon	pepper	1 mL
1 tablespoon	salad oil	15 mL
1 tablespoon	wine vinegar	15 mL
4	chicken breasts, boneless and skinless	4

Mix together all of the ingredients, except the chicken breasts, in a large bowl. Add the chicken breasts, tossing to coat completely, and let marinate for about 1 hour. Remove chicken breasts, reserving marinade.

Place chicken on upper grill over medium heat. Turn and baste with the reserved marinade. Continue cooking until fork-tender and golden brown.

Cooking Time: 8 minutes on each side

Serves 4

Japanese Chicken

Quick and easy, not too many ingredients, and great flavour!

4	chicken breasts, boneless and skinless	4
1 cup	Japanese or light soya sauce	250 mL
½ teaspoon	grated fresh ginger	2 mL
	Juice of one lemon	

Cut the chicken into 1-inch (2.5 cm) pieces. Mix together in a medium bowl the soya sauce, ginger and lemon juice. Add the chicken pieces and marinate for 2 hours, tossing occasionally.

Thread onto small wooden or bamboo skewers and place on upper grill over medium heat, turning and basting with the reserved marinade, until golden.

Cooking Time: 8 minutes

Serves 4

Lemon Chicken

There are many recipes for Lemon Chicken, but this is our favourite.

4	chicken breasts, boneless and skinless	4
¼ cup	lemon juice	50 mL
1 teaspoon	grated lemon peel	5 mL
1 tablespoon	chopped fresh parsley	15 mL
½ teaspoon	salt	2 mL
¼ teaspoon	pepper	1 mL

Place the chicken breasts in a pan. Mix together remaining ingredients. Pour over the chicken and turn to coat completely. Let marinate for 1 hour.

Place on upper grill over medium heat, until white and fluffy inside with no trace of pink showing.

Cooking Time: 8 minutes on each side

Serves 4

HINT: If a recipe calls for grated lemon peel, be sure to grate only the thin top layer of the skin, called zest. The inner white part is bitter.

Hawaiian Stuffed Chicken Breasts

This dish not only tastes wonderful, it's also attractive to serve.

4	chicken breasts, boneless and skinless	4
	Salt to taste	
	Pepper to taste	
2	green onions	2
1	papaya	1
1	tomato	1

Lay the chicken breasts out flat and cut two slits, slanted and about ½ inch (1 cm) deep, down the length of the breasts. Sprinkle lightly with salt and pepper.

Cut off the white part of the green onion and cut several 3-inch-long (8 cm) pieces of green tops. Lay a couple of these in one of the slits in each of the chicken breasts.

Peel the papaya and cut into ¼-inch-wide (5 mm) strips, about 3 inches (8 cm) long. Lay one of these in the other slit in each of the chicken breasts.

Cut the tomato crosswise into four ¼-inch-wide (5 mm) slices. Cut tomato slices in half and remove the seeds and mushy part of tomato. Lay these strips in the centre of each chicken breast, between the slits.

Fold long sides of chicken breast over to the centre. Wrap individually in plastic wrap and refrigerate for 30 minutes. (This will keep the chicken breasts together.) Remove the plastic wrap from the chicken breasts just before cooking.

Place on the upper grill over medium heat, turning once.

Let the breasts rest for a few minutes before slicing. Cut into ¾-inch (2 cm) slices across the width and fan slightly to reveal the colourful stuffing inside.

Cooking Time: 8 minutes on each side

Serves 4

Papaya is a juicy fruit with smooth, orange-yellow flesh. The size of a small melon, it has a similar seed-filled cavity, though it is really a berry. Purchase fruit that is greenish-yellow and yields gently to pressure.

Spinach-Stuffed Chicken

6-pound	roasting chicken	2.5 kg
6	slices bread, cubed	6
½ cup	dry sherry	125 mL
2 tablespoons	vegetable oil	25 mL
1	medium onion, chopped	1
2	garlic cloves, chopped	2
1	package (10 oz./284 g) frozen chopped spinach, thawed and drained	1
½ cup	toasted pine nuts	125 mL
½ cup	grated Parmesan cheese	125 mL
½ teaspoon	salt	2 mL
¼ teaspoon	pepper	1 mL

Rinse the chicken under cold running water and pat dry with paper towels.

Place bread cubes in a medium bowl and pour in the sherry, tossing to mix in. Heat the oil in a skillet and add the onion and garlic, cooking until tender. Add the spinach and simmer for 5 minutes. Remove from heat and add to the bowl of bread cubes. Mix in, adding the pine nuts, Parmesan cheese, salt and pepper.

Stuff spinach mixture into the cavity of the chicken. Close the openings with small skewers. Tie the legs together and the wings over the breast with heavy string. Rub chicken all over with oil.

Insert spit rod through the centre of the bird and secure with holding forks. Place on rotisserie over medium-low indirect heat. You may also place on the upper grill over medium-low indirect heat, turning occasionally. Chicken is done when leg moves easily.

If chicken seems to be drying out, baste with a little melted butter.

Cooking Time: 1 to 1½ hours

Serves 6

Cornish Hens in Lime

We love Cornish hens and buy them by the boxful. Though I have many different recipes, this is one we really enjoy.

2	Rock Cornish hens, about 1½ pounds (750 g) each	2
½ cup	lime juice	125 mL
1 tablespoon	vegetable oil	15 mL
1	small onion, minced	1
2	garlic cloves, crushed	2
1 tablespoon	chopped cilantro	15 mL
½ teaspoon	salt	2 mL
¼ teaspoon	black pepper or cayenne pepper	1 mL

Rinse the hens under cold running water and pat dry with paper towels. Cut the hens in half with kitchen shears.

Prepare the marinade by mixing together the remaining ingredients. Marinate hens for 1 hour.

Place the hens on the upper grill, cut side down, over medium-low heat. Baste with the marinade. Turn and cook the other side halfway through cooking time.

Cooking Time: 12 minutes for each side

Serves 4

Asian Quail

These delicate little birds are a real treat and meant to be eaten with your hands.

6	quail	6
2 tablespoons	vegetable oil	25 mL
2 tablespoons	soya sauce	25 mL
1 tablespoon	oyster sauce	15 mL
1 tablespoon	fish sauce	15 mL
2 tablespoons	brown sugar	25 mL
1	garlic clove, crushed	1

Cut quail in half lengthwise.

Mix together remaining ingredients in a medium bowl. Add the quail and toss to coat completely. Marinate for 2 hours.

Place quail on upper grill over medium heat, turning halfway through cooking time.

Cooking Time: 8 minutes each side

Serves 6

Oyster sauce is a rich brown sauce made from oysters cooked in salt and soya sauce. It can be bought in Asian and specialty food stores.

Fish
and
Shellfish

Grilled Whole Salmon with Herbs

3-pound	whole salmon, filleted	1.5 kg
	Lemon juice	
2	large stalks fresh dillweed	2
¼ cup	dry white wine	50 mL
1 tablespoon	lemon juice	15 mL
1 tablespoon	chopped shallots	15 mL
½ teaspoon	dried tarragon	2 mL
½ teaspoon	dried dill	2 mL
½ teaspoon	salt	2 mL
	Lemon wedges (for garnish)	

Rinse fish under cold running water and pat dry with paper towels. Lay out in the centre of a large piece of heavy-duty aluminum foil. Fold up the sides slightly. Sprinkle the cavity of the salmon with lemon juice and place stalks of dill inside.

In a small saucepan, mix together the remaining ingredients, except lemon wedges. Bring to a boil and simmer until reduced by half. Pour over the fish and close the foil, sealing securely. Place on a baking sheet.

Place on the upper grill over medium heat, with the lid lowered, until fish flakes easily with a fork or flesh is opaque. Serve with juice from the foil package and garnish with fresh lemon wedges.

Cooking Time: 30 minutes

Serves 6

HINT: Stuffings and marinades for seafood recipes can often be mixed and matched. For instance, try the recipe for Grilled Whole Salmon with Herbs with trout. Interchange the recipes for swordfish and shark steaks.

Seafood-Stuffed Flounder

The stuffing tastes just as good as the flounder. An impressive way to serve fish.

2	dressed flounder (with head and tail), 1 pound (500 g) each, cut in half	2
¼ cup	butter	50 mL
½ cup	finely chopped onion	125 mL
½ cup	finely chopped carrot	125 mL
½ cup	finely chopped celery	125 mL
2	garlic cloves, finely chopped	2
2 tablespoons	chopped parsley	25 mL
½ teaspoon	salt	2 mL
¼ teaspoon	pepper	1 mL
1½ cups	soft bread crumbs	375 mL
½ pound	cooked shrimp, coarsely chopped	250 g
½ pound	crab meat	250 g
2 tablespoons	lemon juice	25 mL
1 tablespoon	oil	15 mL
	Lemon or lime slices (for garnish)	

Melt the butter in a medium skillet and add the onion, carrot, celery and garlic. Sauté over medium heat until vegetables are tender. Remove from heat and add seasonings and bread crumbs. Stir in shrimp and crab meat.

Rinse fish and pat dry. Cut a slit along the backbone. Slice a pocket on both sides of the lengthwise cut. Fill the cavity of each fish with stuffing.

Mix together the lemon juice and oil and rub all over the fish.

Place in a hinged grill basket or place the flounder on the upper grill over medium heat until fish flakes easily with a fork.

To serve the flounder, cut across the top of the fish to the backbone. Continue cutting around the outside edge of the fish. Lift off the meat and stuffing. Slide a knife under the backbone and lift it away from the fish. Cut meat into serving pieces. Garnish with lemon or lime slices.

Cooking Time: 20 minutes

Serves 4

Red Snapper Stuffed with Seasoned Rice

4-pound	red snapper	2 kg

STUFFING

¼ cup	butter	50 mL
2 tablespoons	chopped onion	25 mL
2	garlic cloves, crushed	2
½ cup	pine nuts	125 mL
1 cup	cooked rice	250 mL
2 tablespoons	chopped fresh parsley or cilantro	25 mL
2 teaspoons	grated lemon peel	10 mL

In a skillet, melt the butter. Sauté the onions, garlic and pine nuts until the nuts are browned. Add the remaining stuffing ingredients and mix together well.

Spoon mixture into the fish. Pull fish together and insert toothpicks or short skewers every inch. Lace between the toothpicks with heavy string, if necessary, pulling fish tightly together. Rub the fish all over with oil.

Place on the upper grill over medium heat until fish flakes easily with a fork.

Cooking Time: 20 minutes

Serves 6 to 8

HINT: It is easier to remove skewers from meat or fish if you coat them with a little vegetable oil before inserting.

Sole in Parchment

This method of cooking in parchment keeps all the juices and flavour together with the fish. It is also not as messy to serve.

2 tablespoons	butter	25 mL
¼ pound	mushrooms, sliced	125 g
1 cup	whipping cream	250 mL
4	sole fillets	4
	Salt to taste	
	Pepper to taste	
2	small carrots, grated	2

Melt the butter in a skillet over moderate heat and add the sliced mushrooms. Cook for about 3 minutes, stirring occasionally. Increase heat to high and add the cream. Bring to a boil and cook until the cream is reduced to ½ cup (125 mL). Set aside.

Cut four 12-inch (30 cm) squares of parchment paper. Place a sole fillet on half of each square and sprinkle with the salt and pepper. Spoon mushroom mixture over the fillets and top each with one-quarter of the carrots. Fold the other half of the paper over each fillet and fold edges of paper over two or three times. Turn ends under to seal.

Place on upper grill over low heat until paper is slightly browned.

Cut a slice in top of each packet to let steam escape before serving.

Cooking Time: 10 minutes

Serves 4

Sea Bass with Dill and Horseradish

An unusual combination of seasonings that doesn't overpower the flavour of the sea bass. Try this with other kinds of fish.

4	sea bass, whole or filleted	4
¼ cup	butter	50 mL
1	garlic clove, crushed	1
1 teaspoon	dried dill	5 mL
1 teaspoon	horseradish	5 mL
¼ teaspoon	salt	1 mL
	Few grindings of pepper	

Lay the fish out on a platter. Mix together the remaining ingredients, blending well into a paste.

Spread paste on one side of fillets or in middle of whole fish. Refrigerate for 30 minutes.

Place on upper grill over medium heat until centre is opaque and fish flakes easily with a fork. Do not turn over.

Cooking Time: 15 to 20 minutes

Serves 4

HINT: To prevent fish from sticking to your grill, brush the grill with some vegetable oil or line it with lettuce leaves, placing fish on top.

Monkfish in Caper Sauce

Caper Sauce can be used with virtually any kind of fish. Leftover sauce can be stored in the refrigerator for a couple of weeks.

4	monkfish, ½ pound (250 g) each, filleted	4
1 tablespoon	oil	15 mL

CAPER SAUCE

2 tablespoons	olive oil	25 mL
2 tablespoons	butter	25 mL
1 teaspoon	minced onion	5 mL
2	garlic cloves, crushed	2
3	sun-dried tomatoes, chopped	3
1 teaspoon	dried tarragon	5 mL
1 tablespoon	capers, drained	15 mL
	Salt to taste	
	Pepper to taste	
½ cup	dry sherry	125 mL

Rub the fillets with oil and place on the upper grill over medium heat until fish flakes easily with a fork.

Combine the sauce ingredients in a small saucepan and bring to a simmer. Pour over grilled fish when ready to serve.

Cooking Time: 20 minutes

Serves 4

Swordfish Steaks
with Pesto

4	swordfish steaks, ½ pound (250 g) each	4
	Pesto Sauce (page 173)	

Spread the top of the swordfish steaks with some of the Pesto Sauce and refrigerate for 30 minutes.

Place fish on the upper grill over medium heat, with Pesto side up, until the centre is opaque. Do not turn over.

Cooking Time: 10 minutes

Serves 4

Shark Steaks with Garlic Lemon Paste

4	shark steaks, ½ pound (250 g) each	4
	Juice of one lemon	
1 tablespoon	lemon juice	15 mL
1	garlic clove, crushed	1
½ teaspoon	dried basil	2 mL
¼ teaspoon	salt	1 mL
	Few grindings of black pepper	

Place the shark steaks on a platter and sprinkle the lemon juice over top. Set aside.

Combine the remaining ingredients into a paste. Spread over top of the steaks and refrigerate for 30 minutes.

Place the shark steaks on the upper grill over medium heat, with paste side up, until centre is opaque. Do not turn over.

Cooking Time: 10 minutes

Serves 4

Seafood Jambalaya

This recipe is straight from Cajun country.

10	bacon slices, diced	10
1	medium onion, chopped	1
½ cup	sliced celery	125 mL
2	garlic cloves, minced	2
1 teaspoon	dried thyme	5 mL
½ teaspoon	cayenne pepper	2 mL
1 teaspoon	salt	5 mL
¼ teaspoon	black pepper	1 mL
1	can tomatoes (28 oz./796 mL)	1
2 cups	peas	500 mL
2 cups	cooked rice	500 mL
1 pound	scallops	500 g
1 pound	shrimp, peeled	500 g

In a large skillet, on the lower burner over medium heat, cook bacon, onion, celery and garlic until just tender. Add the remaining ingredients and stir gently. Cover and simmer until the scallops are white and fluffy and the shrimp are pink. Serve immediately.

Cooking Time: 15 minutes

Serves 4

Seafood Brochettes

This is a good recipe to use to introduce people to shark steak. They probably won't recognize it and will have to ask what it is.

½ cup	olive oil	125 mL
½ cup	lemon juice	125 mL
½ teaspoon	salt	2 mL
	Fresh ground pepper	
4	garlic cloves, crushed	4
1 teaspoon	finely minced fresh ginger	5 mL
1 pound	large shrimp	500 g
1 pound	shark steaks, boned and cubed	500 g
2	cans artichoke hearts (each 14 oz./398 mL)	2

In a large bowl, mix together the olive oil, lemon juice, salt, pepper, garlic and ginger.

Add the shrimp, shark and artichoke hearts to the marinade and toss to coat completely. Marinate in refrigerator for 2 hours.

Thread the seafood and artichoke hearts onto wooden or bamboo skewers, alternating them as you go. Skewer the shrimp lengthwise, through the centre, making the heads double up against the tails.

Place on the upper grill of the barbecue, over medium heat, turning once.

Cooking Time: 5 to 10 minutes

Serve on a bed of rice.

Serves 4

Grilled Shellfish

Proportions depend on whether you are serving the shellfish as an appetizer or as a main course. Four for each person serves as an appetizer, approximately 10 or 12 as a main course.

The following may be served individually, or combine some of each for a mixed grill.

Blue Point oysters
Razor clams
Littleneck clams
Mussels
Bay scallops
Seasoned Butter

Wash the shellfish. Place on the lower grill over medium-high heat. After about 5 minutes, they will start to open. Remove and discard the top shells. Move to the upper grill and spoon in a little of the seasoned butter. Continue cooking for another 3 minutes. Discard any shellfish that do not open.

HINT: Clams should be alive when they are bought. The shells should be closed or shut tightly when tapped. Shucked clams should be plump, shiny and fresh smelling.

Mussels should be bought fresh in the shells. They should be unbroken and tightly closed or shut tightly when tapped.

Scallops should be creamy pink with a slightly sweet odour. Bay scallops are smaller than sea scallops.

Shrimp should have firm-textured meat. Shells may be light gray, brownish pink or red.

Seasoned Butters

Melt butter and add remaining ingredients. Keep warm until ready to use. Quantities here are for about 16 shellfish.

LEMON BUTTER

½ cup	butter	125 mL
2 tablespoons	lemon juice	25 mL
	Salt and pepper to taste	

GARLIC BUTTER

½ cup	butter	125 mL
2	garlic cloves, crushed	2
1 tablespoon	chopped parsley	15 mL
	Salt and pepper to taste	

ALMOND BUTTER

½ cup	butter	125 mL
1	garlic clove, crushed	1
½ cup	ground toasted almonds	125 mL
	Salt and pepper to taste	

PINE NUT BUTTER

½ cup	butter	125 mL
¼ cup	toasted pine nuts, finely chopped	50 mL
	Salt and pepper to taste	

Shrimp In Shell

2 pounds	medium shrimp, unpeeled	1 kg

Wash the shrimp under cold running water. Place on lower grill over medium heat, turning once, until pink.

Cooking Time: 4 or 5 minutes

Serve with seafood dipping sauces such as Rémoulade (page 180) or Cocktail Sauce (page 181).

Serves 4

Peppered Prawns

Prawns are somewhat the same as shrimp, which may be substituted.

2 pounds	large prawns (or shrimp)	1 kg
¼ cup	lemon juice	50 mL
3	garlic cloves, crushed	3
1½ teaspoons	black peppercorns, cracked	7 mL
1½ teaspoons	red peppercorns, cracked	7 mL

Shell the prawns, leaving the tail on. Remove vein on back.

Mix together the remaining ingredients. Add the prawns and marinate for 1 or 2 hours.

Remove the prawns, reserving the marinade.

Place the prawns on a well-oiled griddle, on lower grill over high heat. Cook, drizzling with marinade, and turning until pink.

Cooking Time: 5 minutes

Serves 4

Florida Shrimp

This combination is a tasty surprise for your palate.

2 pounds	medium shrimp, shelled	1 kg
½ cup	lime juice	125 mL
1	garlic clove, crushed	1
1 tablespoon	chopped cilantro	15 mL
	Fresh ground pepper	
1	can smoked oysters	1

Rinse the shrimp under cold running water and pat dry with paper towels.

Mix together the remaining ingredients, except the smoked oysters. Add the shrimp and marinate for 1 or 2 hours.

Remove the shrimp, reserving the marinade. Wrap each shrimp around a smoked oyster and secure with toothpick.

Place on the upper grill over medium heat, turning once, until pink. Place on a platter and drizzle the reserved marinade over top.

Cooking Time: 5 minutes

Serves 4

Scallops Wrapped in Green Onion

This is an attractive way to serve scallops, and they have a wonderful flavour.

2 pounds	scallops	1 kg
½ cup	lime juice	125 mL
1 tablespoon	chopped fresh cilantro or parsley	15 mL
1	garlic clove, crushed	1
½ teaspoon	garam masala	2 mL
	Green onions	

Rinse the scallops under cold running water, drain well and pat dry with paper towels.

Mix together the lime juice, cilantro, garlic and garam masala. Add the scallops and marinate for 2 hours.

Remove the scallops from the marinade. Cut strips of green from the onion. Wrap a strip of green leaf around each scallop and thread onto wooden skewers.

Place on the upper grill over medium heat, turning frequently, until opaque.

Cooking Time: 5 minutes

Serves 4 to 6

Grilled Whole Lobster

1	lobster per person,	1
	1 to 1½ pounds (500 to 750 g) each	

STUFFING (PER LOBSTER)

2 tablespoons	dried bread crumbs	25 mL
1 teaspoon	lemon juice	5 mL

BASTING SAUCE AND
DIPPING SAUCE FOR TWO

½ cup	melted butter	125 mL
¼ cup	lemon juice	50 mL
½ teaspoon	salt	2 mL
2 tablespoons	chopped fresh parsley	25 mL
1	garlic clove, crushed	1

Prepare the lobster: With a sharp knife, sever the vein at the base of the neck, underneath the shell. Place the lobster on its back and, with your hand wrapped in a towel, hold it firmly in place by the head. Draw the knife from the head down through the abdomen, thus allowing the lobster to lie flat and evenly expose the meat. Discard the stomach (hard sac near the head) and intestine that runs from it through the middle of the abdomen to the tail.

Remove the red coral and green liver or tomalley. Place these in a small bowl and mix together with the bread crumbs and lemon juice. Replace in the cavity.

Combine the basting sauce ingredients. Brush on the lobster meat and place in a hinged basket. (If you do not have a hinged basket, proceed without one.) Place on the upper grill over medium heat, shell side up, for 8 to 10 minutes. Turn and grill for an additional 8 minutes until lightly browned and tender. Before serving, brush again with the basting sauce. Serve the remainder on the side for dipping.

Be careful not to overcook, as it will toughen the meat and ruin the flavour.

Cooking Time: 8 minutes on each side

Stuffed Lobster Tails

This may be served as an appetizer or together with steak for Surf 'n' Turf.

½ cup	soya sauce	125 mL
1 tablespoon	sugar	15 mL
1	can water chestnuts, drained (10 oz./284 g)	1
2	lobster tails, 8 oz. (250 g) each	2
10	strips bacon	10

Mix together the soya sauce and sugar in a small deep bowl, stirring to dissolve sugar. Add the water chestnuts. Toss gently to cover. Marinate for a couple of hours, stirring frequently. Drain.

Wash the lobster tails and remove shell by cutting the underside, lengthwise, with scissors. Pound tail flat until it is ¼ to ½ inch (5 mm to 1 cm) thick. Cut lengthwise into strips 1 to 1½ inches (2.5 to 4 cm) wide. Wrap each water chestnut with a strip of lobster tail and then a strip of bacon. Secure with a toothpick. Each lobster tail will make 4 or 5 roll-ups.

Barbecue on upper grill over medium heat on a sheet of perforated foil (to prevent flare-ups from bacon) until bacon is crisp and lobster is puffy white.

Cooking Time: 15 minutes

Serves 4 to 6

Vegetables and Rice

Stuffed Artichokes

Stuffed Artichokes are a meal in themselves, so don't serve them as a side vegetable. We have found that a light seafood dish, bruschetta or a salad are a great accompaniment and balance out the meal nicely.

4	medium artichokes	4
2 cups	soft bread crumbs	500 mL
1	medium onion, finely minced	1
1 tablespoon	summer savory, crushed	15 mL
1 cup	grated Parmesan cheese	250 mL
1 tablespoon	chopped parsley	15 mL
	Salt to taste	
	Pepper to taste	
	Milk	
½ cup	butter	125 mL
1 tablespoon	lemon juice	15 mL

Prepare the artichokes: Hold the stem end and plunge up and down a few times in a deep dish of salted water. Drain well. Cut off the stems and remove the bottom row of small leaves. With scissors, cut off the top ¼ inch (5 mm) of each leaf.

Prepare the dressing: Mix together the bread crumbs, onion, savory, Parmesan cheese, parsley, salt and pepper. Add enough milk to moisten slightly.

Separate the artichoke leaves slightly and push dressing down in between the outer leaves. (Close to the centre, the leaves are too compact to get any dressing in.)

Place the stuffed artichokes in a baking dish or roasting pan with ½ inch (1 cm) of water in the bottom. Cover and place on upper grill over low heat. You may also use medium indirect heat. The artichokes are done when the leaves come away easily.

Cooking Time: 45 minutes

Melt the butter and stir in the lemon juice. Pour into 4 individual serving dishes. Serve on the side with the stuffed artichokes.

To eat, the leaves are dipped, one at a time, in the lemon butter. The lower end of the leaf is pulled through the teeth, removing the soft portion. Discard the leaf. Closer to the centre, more of each leaf is soft and edible. When you get to the soft, fuzzy centre, scrape it out and discard it. This is the choke and it is appropriately named — that is exactly what will happen if you attempt to eat it! The remaining heart can be cut into pieces, dipped in the butter and eaten. It is the best part!

Serves 4

HINT: When choosing artichokes, look for tightly packed leaves and fresh green colour. Drizzle with a bit of water before sealing in plastic bags and refrigerating, to help them last longer.

Asparagus with Saffron Sauce

2 cups	plain yogourt	500 mL
2 teaspoons	honey mustard	10 mL
Pinch	saffron threads	Pinch
¼ teaspoon	ground cumin	1 mL
¼ teaspoon	salt	1 mL
2 pounds	asparagus	1 kg

Line a strainer with cheesecloth and place strainer over a bowl. Pour the yogourt into the strainer and let sit at room temperature for about ½ hour, stirring occasionally.

Pour thickened yogourt into a bowl and mix in the honey mustard, saffron threads, cumin and salt. Cover and set aside until needed. Refrigerate if it is going to be more than an hour.

Remove the tough stem ends of the asparagus by bending each spear gently toward the end. It will break where the tough end stops. Place spears on a sheet of aluminum foil, sealing securely. Place on upper grill over medium heat until tender.

Place the asparagus on a serving platter. Pour yogourt mixture over top and serve immediately.

Cooking Time: 10 minutes

Serves 6 to 8

HINT: Asparagus should have firm, straight stalks, bright green with closed, compact tips. Buy ones that are uniform in size so they will all be done cooking at the same time. The thickness of the stalks has no relationship to tenderness, though short spears are more tender than long ones. To store, wrap ends in moist paper towel or stand in a couple of inches of water, loosely covered and refrigerated. To prepare, break off the woody end by bending until it snaps in two. Leave the stalks whole or cut into pieces.

Green Beans Amandine

1 pound	green beans	500 g
	Salt to taste	
	Pepper to taste	
3 tablespoons	butter	50 mL
¼ cup	slivered almonds	50 mL

Snap off the ends of the beans and wash well. You may leave them whole or French them (cut into slivers lengthwise). Place beans in a pot of boiling water and place on middle grill over high heat to simmer until tender. Drain well and season with salt and pepper.

While the beans are cooking, melt the butter in a small skillet over medium heat and add the almonds. Toss and cook until lightly toasted. Keep warm.

Place the beans in a serving dish and top with the buttered almonds. They may be served this way or tossed lightly.

Cooking Time: 20 minutes

Serves 4

Chinese Long Beans

A lot of people have never tasted Chinese long beans. They have a wonderful texture, crisper than regular green beans.

½ pound	Chinese long beans or green beans	250 g
1 tablespoon	sesame oil	15 mL
1 teaspoon	soya sauce	5 mL
1 teaspoon	toasted sesame seeds	5 mL

Trim beans and cut into 6-inch (15 cm) pieces. Lay on a sheet of aluminum foil and bring up the sides and ends, sealing securely.

Place on the upper rack over medium heat until just tender.

Meanwhile, mix together the remaining ingredients. Toss with the cooked beans.

Cooking Time: 20 minutes

Serves 4

Sesame Broccoli

2 pounds	broccoli, cut into flowerets	1 kg
¼ cup	water	50 mL
1 tablespoon	soya sauce	15 mL
1 tablespoon	sesame oil	15 mL
2 tablespoons	butter	25 mL
1	can (8 oz./227 g) sliced water chestnuts, drained	1
1 tablespoon	toasted sesame seeds	15 mL

Place water, soya sauce, sesame oil and butter in wok on lower grill over high heat and bring to a boil. Add the broccoli and water chestnuts and stir-fry until broccoli is tender-crisp. Toss with sesame seeds and serve.

Cooking Time: 10 minutes

Serves 8

Brussels Sprouts
with Caraway

The caraway gives this dish a wonderful flavour, so even those who don't care for brussels sprouts may change their mind.

1 pound	brussels sprouts	500 g
	Lemon juice	
	Salt	
	Pepper	
	Caraway seeds	
3 tablespoons	butter	50 mL

Cut the stem ends from the sprouts and cut a shallow "x" in the bottom of each sprout to ensure even cooking. Lay on a sheet of aluminum foil and sprinkle lightly with lemon juice, salt, pepper and caraway seeds to taste. Dot with the butter. Bring up the ends of the foil and seal securely.

Place on the upper grill over medium heat until fork-tender.

Cooking Time: 10 minutes

Serves 4

HINT: When buying brussels sprouts, choose the smallest ones with bright green leaves and tight, compact heads.

Cognac Carrots

A great way to give carrots a real boost in flavour.

⅓ cup	butter	75 mL
4 teaspoons	sugar	20 mL
2 pounds	carrots, peeled and sliced	1 kg
	Salt to taste	
	Pepper to taste	
⅓ cup	cognac or dry sherry	75 mL
	Chopped fresh parsley	

Place the butter and sugar in a foil dish and place on barbecue for a few minutes until butter is melted. Remove from heat, stir slightly, add the carrots and toss to coat. Sprinkle with salt and pepper and cognac. Cover with foil.

Place on upper grill over medium heat until tender. Sprinkle with chopped parsley before serving.

Cooking Time: 30 minutes

Serves 6

Orange Cauliflower

I use ice cubes when cooking vegetables in foil, as they are more manageable than water. The ice cubes melt gradually and moisten the cauliflower.

1	head cauliflower, cut into flowerets	1
¼ cup	butter	50 mL
	Juice of one orange	
1 tablespoon	chopped fresh cilantro or parsley	15 mL
½ teaspoon	cumin	2 mL

Place the cauliflower on a sheet of aluminum foil. Top with a couple of ice cubes, bring up the sides of the foil and seal securely.

Place on the upper grill over medium heat, until fork-tender.

Meanwhile, melt the butter in a small saucepan and add the remaining ingredients. Simmer over very low heat until cauliflower is cooked. Remove the cooked cauliflower to a serving bowl and toss with the warm sauce.

Cooking Time: 10 minutes

Serves 4

HINT: To lessen the odour of cooking cauliflower or cabbage, add lemon juice to the water.

Corn-on-the-Cob

Peel back part of the husk from each cob of corn and remove the silk. Butter the kernels and close up again. Place on the lower grill over medium heat, turning occasionally.

An alternative method is to remove husks and silk and soak cobs in cold water for 10 minutes. Shake off excess water and wrap in foil, individually, twisting the ends.

Place on the lower grill over medium heat, turning occasionally.

Cooking Time: 15 minutes

HINT: If you need butter in a hurry and have forgotten to remove it from the refrigerator, grate it to bring it to room temperature quickly.

Kohlrabi in
Dill Sauce

Kohlrabi is one of my favourite vegetables, though I sometimes find it difficult to obtain. The best solution was to grow it myself!

1 pound	cleaned kohlrabi	500 g
3 tablespoons	butter	50 mL
½ cup	sour cream	125 mL
1 tablespoon	dried dill	15 mL
1 tablespoon	lemon juice	15 mL
	Salt to taste	
	Pepper to taste	

Cut the ends off the kohlrabi, peel and cut into ¼-inch (5 mm) slices. Bring a pot of lightly salted water to a boil on the lower grill over high heat. Add the kohlrabi and continue to boil until fork-tender. Drain.

Melt the butter in a saucepan, add the kohlrabi and toss to coat. Stir in remaining ingredients. Cook for another couple of minutes until sauce is heated. Serve immediately.

Cooking Time: 10 minutes after water comes to a boil

Serves 6

Kohlrabi is German for "cabbage-turnip". It is a member of the cabbage family but milder in taste with a firm body like the turnip.

Stuffed Peppers

The capers and anchovies give this dish an interesting flavour.

4	large green peppers	4
2 cups	hot cooked rice	500 mL
2 tablespoons	butter	25 mL
1	large tomato, peeled, seeded and chopped	1
6	crushed anchovy fillets	6
½ teaspoon	crushed dried basil	2 mL
½ teaspoon	salt	2 mL
	Fresh ground pepper	
2 tablespoons	capers	25 mL
½ cup	shredded mozzarella or Cheddar cheese	125 mL

Slice off the stem end of each pepper and remove the seeds and white ribs. Place each pepper, cut side up, on a double-thickness of aluminum foil.

Mix together the rice, butter, tomato, anchovies and seasonings, adding the capers last to avoid crushing them. Stuff the peppers with the rice mixture and place the shredded cheese on top. Bring up the sides of the foil and wrap loosely but securely.

Place on the upper grill over medium heat.

Cooking Time: 15 minutes

Serves 4

HINT: The best way to seed a tomato is to cut it in half crosswise and gently squeeze each half with your hand.

Stuffed Baked Potatoes with Bacon and Cheese

These can be prepared ahead of time and frozen. Lay out on a cookie sheet and freeze, then layer in an airtight container. Handy to have on hand when you don't feel like cooking.

4	large baking potatoes	4
2 tablespoons	butter (or more)	25 mL
¼ cup	sour cream	50 mL
2 tablespoons	grated Parmesan cheese	25 mL
2 tablespoons	chopped chives	25 mL
4	slices crisp bacon, crumbled	4
	Salt to taste	
	Pepper to taste	
	Melted butter	
	Paprika	

Scrub the potatoes and pierce a few times with a fork. Place on the upper rack over medium heat, with the lid down, until well cooked. Cooking time will be reduced if potatoes are wrapped in foil.

Cooking Time: Approximately 1 hour

Slice potatoes in half lengthwise and remove pulp to a bowl, being careful not to damage the skins. Mash pulp with the butter, sour cream, grated cheese, chives and bacon. Salt and pepper to taste. Mound back into potato skins.

Drizzle with melted butter and sprinkle with paprika.

Return to upper rack of barbecue and heat through.

Serves 4

HINT: If you want a crisper skin on a baked potato, if stuffing for instance, don't wrap it in foil and bake it a little longer.

Sliced Baked Potatoes with Herbs and Cheese

Try a bit of cumin as a seasoning with this dish for a different taste.

4	baking potatoes	4
	Salt to taste	
	Pepper to taste	
3 tablespoons	melted butter	50 mL
1 tablespoon	chopped chives	15 mL
1 tablespoon	parsley	15 mL
1 teaspoon	dried thyme	5 mL
¼ cup	shredded Cheddar cheese	50 mL
2 tablespoons	grated Parmesan cheese	25 mL

Peel the potatoes and cut into thin slices, but not quite all the way through. Fan the potatoes slightly and sprinkle with salt and pepper. Drizzle with melted butter. Top with the herbs and wrap loosely in foil. Place on the upper grill over medium heat, with the lid down, until fork-tender.

Cooking Time: 40 minutes

Remove the foil and sprinkle with the two cheeses. Continue to bake for an additional 10 or 15 minutes until the cheeses are melted and lightly browned.

Serves 4

Scalloped Potatoes

3 cups	thinly sliced peeled potatoes	750 mL
¼ cup	flour	50 mL
½ cup	butter	125 mL
¼ cup	chopped chives or onion	50 mL
1¼ cups	milk	300 mL
1 teaspoon	salt	5 mL
½ teaspoon	paprika	2 mL
¼ teaspoon	dry mustard	1 mL

Grease a 10-inch square (3 L) baking dish. Place an overlapping layer of potatoes on the bottom. Sprinkle with one-third of the flour, dots of butter and chopped chives. Repeat for three layers.

Heat the milk and add salt, paprika and mustard. Pour over the potatoes. Cover with lid or aluminum foil.

Place on upper grill over medium heat, with the lid down.

Cooking Time: 1 hour

Serves 4 to 6

Parisienne Potatoes

My favourite method of preparing potatoes.

8	large potatoes, peeled	8
⅓ cup	butter	75 mL
	Salt	
	Fresh ground pepper	
2 tablespoons	parsley	25 mL

Scoop out balls of potato with melon-baller. Place potato balls in a bowl of cold water and let stand for 10 minutes or until ready to cook. Drain and dry on paper towels.

In a large skillet on lower grill, melt butter over medium-high heat until it begins to foam. Add potatoes and cook, uncovered, stirring frequently. When potatoes are tender and golden brown, season with salt, pepper and parsley and serve.

Cooking Time: 30 minutes

Serves 4

If you don't want to waste the leftover bits of potato, store what's left in a bowl of cold water in the refrigerator. The next day you can cut it up into small pieces and fry it up, using the same method, for lunch. It may not look as nice, but it tastes just as good. You may also make Potato Pancakes (page 135) or Hash Browns (page 56) out of the pieces.

Potato Pancakes or Latkes

4	medium potatoes	4
2	eggs	2
1	medium onion	1
3 tablespoons	flour	50 mL
1 teaspoon	salt	5 mL
¼ teaspoon	pepper	1 mL
	Cooking oil	

Peel and dice the potatoes. Toss everything, except the cooking oil, into a food processor and blend until mixture is smooth and there are no large lumps of potato.

Preheat a large skillet or griddle over high heat for about 10 minutes. Reduce heat to medium-high and oil the griddle well. Pour on the batter, about ½ cupful (125 mL) per pancake, and flatten gently. Turn when golden brown on the bottom and continue cooking until done. Drain on paper towels and keep warm on plate on warming rack.

Serves 4

HINT: To prevent potato from turning black when making potato pancakes, shred them directly into a bowl of cold water. Dry well before proceeding.

Spaghetti Squash with Vegetables

I have been growing spaghetti squash for years in my garden and always have far more than we can eat in twelve months. I usually find myself giving them away to anyone who comes near our house: friends, lost travellers, the chimney sweep, delivery people. I always have to explain what it is and how to cook it. I should probably print out instructions to be handed out with the squash!

1	spaghetti squash, about 3 pounds (1.5 kg)	1
1 tablespoon	olive oil	15 mL
1	garlic clove, crushed	1
½ teaspoon	salt	2 mL
2 cups	chopped fresh tomatoes	500 mL
½ teaspoon	dried basil	2 mL
	Salt and pepper	
2	large carrots, thinly sliced	2
1 cup	snow peas, sliced in half diagonally	250 mL
2 tablespoons	grated Parmesan cheese	25 mL

Pierce squash about six times with a sharp knife. Place on upper grill over medium heat, with the lid down, for about 15 minutes. Turn and continue cooking another 15 minutes.

Pour the olive oil into the bottom of a 2- or 3-quart (2 or 3 L) casserole dish. Mash together the garlic and salt to make a paste. Add this to the olive oil. Add the chopped tomatoes and blend well. Place on middle grill over medium heat for about 10 minutes. Stir in the basil and season to taste with salt and pepper. Set aside.

Place the carrots in a microwave-safe dish and cover with 2 tablespoons (25 mL) water. Cover loosely with waxed paper and microwave on High for 2 minutes. Add snow peas and microwave on High for 1 minute or until vegetables are tender. Let stand for about 5 minutes. Drain off water and add vegetables to tomato mixture.

Cut the spaghetti squash in half and discard the seeds. With a large spoon, pull the squash free from the shell and add to the tomato mixture. Blend well.

Sprinkle with cheese and serve immediately.

Serves 6

When cooked, spaghetti squash comes apart in long strands of flesh. Hence the name.

Stuffed Tomatoes

This is one of my favourite dishes. It is easy to prepare and tastes wonderful.

4	medium firm tomatoes	4
	Salt	
	Pepper	
	Oregano	
4	slices bacon, diced	4
1	medium onion, chopped	1
1 to 1½ cups	shredded mozzarella or Cheddar cheese	250 to 375 mL
	Buttered bread crumbs (page 144)	

Cut a thin slice off the stem end of each tomato and carefully hollow out tomatoes. Sprinkle the inside of each with salt, pepper and oregano to taste.

In a skillet, fry the bacon and drain, retaining one scant tablespoon (15 mL) of grease. Add the chopped onion and cook until just tender. Let cool slightly and spoon mixture into bottom of tomatoes.

Fill each tomato with shredded cheese and top with buttered bread crumbs.

Place on warming rack of barbecue until heated through and cheese has melted.

Cooking Time: 20 minutes

Serves 4

HINT: Keep tomatoes at room temperature for the best flavour. Buy them at varying degrees of ripeness and use the ripest first. Store them stems up, out of the sun.

Baked Green Tomatoes

Everyone in our family anxiously awaits the day when the first green tomatoes are ready to be picked from the garden. From that day forward, green tomatoes are often a part of every menu. We especially like them for breakfast.

3	large green tomatoes	3
½ teaspoon	sugar	2 mL
	Salt to taste	
	Pepper to taste	
1 cup	fresh bread crumbs	250 mL
½ teaspoon	oregano	2 mL
½ teaspoon	dried basil	2 mL
½ teaspoon	dried thyme	2 mL
¼ cup	melted butter	50 mL
⅓ cup	grated Parmesan cheese	75 mL
3 tablespoons	butter	50 mL

Cut tomatoes crosswise in ½-inch (1 cm) slices and overlap in a lightly oiled baking dish. Sprinkle with sugar, salt and pepper.

Mix bread crumbs, oregano, basil and thyme with melted butter. Sprinkle mixture over tomatoes. Top with Parmesan cheese and dot with butter.

Place on upper grill over medium heat, with lid down.

Cooking Time: 30 minutes

Serves 4

HINT: You can make fresh bread crumbs in your blender, tearing each slice of bread into pieces. One slice of bread makes about ½ cup (125 mL) bread crumbs.

Zucchini Bake

If you have a garden, you probably have more zucchini than you know what to do with. This is a tasty way of preparing it.

½ pound	zucchini, peeled and diced	250 g
2 tablespoons	butter	25 mL
1 tablespoon	chopped chives or green onion	15 mL
2	eggs, beaten	2
⅔ cup	milk	150 mL
	Salt to taste	
	Pepper to taste	
	Grated nutmeg	

Boil the zucchini until very soft. Drain well. Mash the zucchini with butter and chives. Add beaten eggs and milk. Season well with salt and pepper.

Pour into a glass deep-dish pie plate and sprinkle top with grated nutmeg.

Place on upper grill over medium heat, with lid down, until just set.

Cooking Time: 15 minutes

Serves 4

Vegetable Kabobs

Use any or all of the vegetables listed.

| Whole mushrooms |
| Tomatoes, cherry or large, firm, cut in wedges |
| Red or green pepper, in large pieces |
| Potatoes, parboiled and chilled |
| Zucchini, in ½-inch (1 cm) slices |
| Baby onions |
| Eggplant, cubed |
| Whole sweet pimiento, in 1-inch (2.5 cm) squares |

BASTE

½ cup	melted butter	125 mL
1	garlic clove, crushed	1
2 teaspoons	tarragon or parsley	10 mL
½ teaspoon	salt	2 mL
¼ teaspoon	pepper	1 mL

Thread the vegetables onto long metal skewers, alternating. Prepare the baste and keep warm on barbecue.

Place kabobs on the lower grill over low heat until the vegetables are tender-crisp, turning and basting frequently.

Cooking Time: 7 minutes

Serves 6

Garbanzo Burgers

These can also be served to vegetarian guests or people on special diets, in lieu of meat. Just add a bun if you're serving hamburgers.

1	can garbanzos (chick peas) (19 oz./540 mL)	1
2	medium carrots, sliced	2
1	small onion, chopped	1
2	eggs	2
½ teaspoon	oregano	2 mL
½ teaspoon	salt	2 mL
¼ teaspoon	pepper	1 mL
1 cup	dried bread crumbs	250 mL

In food processor, combine the drained garbanzos, carrots and onion. Process until garbanzos are smooth and carrots are finely chopped. Add the remaining ingredients and blend well. Shape into 8 round flat patties. Chill in freezer for 20 to 30 minutes to firm up for easier handling.

Place on lightly greased griddle on the upper grill over medium heat, turning halfway through cooking time or when lightly browned on bottom side.

Serve topped with yogourt and shredded carrots.

Cooking Time: 20 minutes

Serves 4 to 6

Garbanzos with Pimiento

¼ cup	olive oil	50 mL
3	garlic cloves, chopped	3
½ cup	chopped onion	125 mL
1 cup	thinly sliced Italian sausage	250 mL
2	cans garbanzos (chick peas) (each 19 oz./540 mL)	2
½ teaspoon	oregano	2 mL
½ cup	pimiento strips	125 mL
	Salt to taste	
	Pepper to taste	

In a large skillet, heat the oil over moderate heat and add the garlic, onion and sausage, cooking until tender. Drain the garbanzos and add to the skillet along with the oregano and pimiento. Heat through and season with salt and pepper.

Serves 8

HINT: One pound (16 oz./500 g) of dry garbanzo beans equals 2 cups (500 mL). One cup (250 mL) of dry beans will yield about 2½ cups (625 mL) cooked beans.

Vegetable Toppings

BUTTERED CRUMB TOPPING

One of my favourite ways to dress up steamed vegetables is to make a topping of buttered crumbs. This is especially good on broccoli, cauliflower, beans and peas.

½ cup	butter	125 mL
1 cup	dried bread crumbs	250 mL

Melt the butter in a small saucepan, brown lightly, and add the dried bread crumbs. Toss and cook for a few minutes over low heat and keep warm until ready to serve.

I usually serve the topping in a side dish for people to help themselves, but you may also pour it over the vegetables in a serving dish.

Serves 4

PINE NUT TOPPING

¼ cup	butter	50 mL
¼ cup	pine nuts	50 mL

Melt the butter in a small pan over moderate heat and add the pine nuts. Toss and cook until the pine nuts are toasted. Keep warm until ready to serve. Pour over vegetables and toss gently.

Serves 4

Florentine Rice

2 cups	cooked long-grain rice	500 mL
1	package (10 oz./284 g) frozen chopped spinach, thawed and drained	1
1 cup	shredded Swiss cheese	250 mL
½ cup	milk	125 mL
1	egg, beaten	1
1 teaspoon	salt	5 mL

Stir together cooked rice and spinach; blend in the remaining ingredients. Place in a 1-quart (1 L) casserole dish.

Place on upper grill over medium heat, with the lid down, until set.

Cooking Time: 15 minutes

Serves 4

Pilaf

½ cup	butter	125 mL
¼ cup	chopped onion	50 mL
2 cups	long-grain rice	500 mL
4 cups	chicken broth	1 L
1 teaspoon	salt	5 mL
½ teaspoon	turmeric	2 mL

In a medium saucepan, melt the butter over moderate heat. Add the onions and cook for a couple of minutes until the onion is tender. Add the rice and sauté until the rice is translucent, making sure not to brown. Mix in the chicken broth and seasonings and bring to a boil.

Place on upper grill over medium heat, cover and simmer until rice is tender and liquid is absorbed. Toss with fork before serving.

Cooking Time: 20 minutes

Serves 8

Orzo and Rice Amandine

Orzo is a pasta shaped like grains of rice. A great combination.

3 cups	water	750 mL
1 tablespoon	chicken Bovril	15 mL
½ cup	orzo	125 mL
1 cup	basmati or long-grain rice	250 mL
1 tablespoon	butter	15 mL
1 teaspoon	salt	5 mL
	Pepper to taste	
¼ cup	chopped fresh parsley	50 mL
½ teaspoon	tarragon	2 mL
2 tablespoons	grated Parmesan cheese	25 mL
¼ cup	toasted slivered almonds	50 mL

Bring the water and chicken Bovril to a boil and add the orzo, rice, butter, salt, pepper, parsley and tarragon.

Place on upper grill over medium heat and simmer until tender and water is absorbed.

Mix in the Parmesan cheese and slivered almonds. Serve immediately.

Cooking Time: 30 minutes

Serves 4

Saffron Rice

4 cups	water	1 L
2 cups	basmati or long-grain rice	500 mL
¼ teaspoon	saffron threads	1 mL
1 cup	hot water	250 mL
¼ cup	melted butter	50 mL
1	small onion, thinly sliced	1
1 tablespoon	finely chopped fresh ginger	15 mL
½ cup	unsalted cashews	125 mL
4	whole cloves	4
1 teaspoon	salt	5 mL
½ teaspoon	turmeric	2 mL
½ cup	lime juice	125 mL
3 tablespoons	chopped cilantro	50 mL

Bring the 4 cups (1 L) of water to a boil in a large saucepan and slowly add the rice. Cook over moderate heat for 10 minutes. Strain the rice through a sieve and set aside.

Soak the saffron threads in the cup (250 mL) of hot water and set aside. Heat the butter over high heat in a large heavy casserole and add the onions, ginger, cashews and cloves. Cook and stir for a couple of minutes. Mix in the rice, salt, turmeric, lime juice and cilantro. Pour in the saffron threads and water and stir gently. Bring to a boil, stirring occasionally. Remove from heat.

Cover with lid or aluminum foil. Place on upper grill over medium heat and cook until rice has absorbed all the liquid. Serve immediately.

Cooking Time: 30 minutes

Serves 8

Seasoned Rice
with Pine Nuts

5 tablespoons	butter	75 mL
1 cup	long-grain rice	250 mL
2 cups	chicken broth	500 mL
1 teaspoon	salt	5 mL
1 cup	finely chopped onion	250 mL
½ cup	pine nuts	125 mL
2 tablespoons	chopped fresh parsley	25 mL

Melt 3 tablespoons (50 mL) butter in a saucepan over moderate heat. Add the rice and stir constantly for a couple of minutes until the rice is no longer opaque. Be careful not to let it brown. Pour in the chicken broth and add the salt. Bring to a boil, stirring occasionally.

Cover the pan tightly and place on upper grill over medium heat for 20 minutes or until the rice has absorbed all the liquid.

In a small skillet, melt the remaining 2 tablespoons (25 mL) of butter and add the onion. Cook over moderate heat until the onions are tender. Add the pine nuts and cook for a couple of minutes longer, stirring, until the pine nuts are lightly browned.

Combine the rice and pine nut mixture and add the parsley. Season to taste.

Cooking Time: 30 minutes

Serves 4

Salads
and
Dressings

Thai Cucumber Salad

1	English cucumber	1
¼ cup	chopped fresh cilantro	50 mL
¼ cup	lime juice	50 mL
2 tablespoons	minced red onion	25 mL
1 teaspoon	sugar	5 mL
2 tablespoons	rice or cider vinegar	25 mL
¼ teaspoon	hot pepper flakes	1 mL
	Lettuce leaves	
¼ cup	chopped hazelnuts	50 mL

Cut cucumber in half lengthwise. Cut into thin slices.

In a medium bowl, combine the cilantro, lime juice, onion, sugar, vinegar and hot pepper flakes. Stir to dissolve sugar. Add the cucumber and toss gently. Cover and refrigerate for at least 1 hour.

When serving, line a bowl or platter with lettuce leaves. Using a slotted spoon, place cucumber mixture in centre. Sprinkle with nuts.

Serves 4

English cucumber is a long, thinner cucumber with fewer and smaller seeds.

Almond Orange Salad

This salad is almost like a dessert. The sugared almonds offset the vinegar so it's an unusual treat for your taste buds.

¼ cup	sliced almonds	50 mL
4 teaspoons	sugar	20 mL
1	head romaine lettuce	1
1	can mandarin oranges, drained (10 oz./284 mL)	1
¼ cup	vegetable oil	50 mL
2 tablespoons	sugar	25 mL
2 tablespoons	vinegar	25 mL
½ teaspoon	salt	2 mL
1 tablespoon	chopped chives	15 mL

Mix together the sliced almonds and sugar in a frypan and stir over low heat until sugar is melted. Spoon onto a sheet of waxed paper and let cool.

Tear the romaine into chunks and place in a large salad bowl. Add the drained mandarin oranges to the top. Break the almond mixture into chunks and add to the salad.

Combine the remaining ingredients and mix together well. Pour the dressing over the salad and toss.

Serves 4

Tabbouleh

This recipe is from the Middle East and is always a real hit. It has many variations and whenever I taste someone else's, it is usually quite different.

½ cup	bulghur (cracked wheat)	125 mL
3	medium tomatoes, finely chopped	3
1 cup	finely chopped fresh parsley	250 mL
1 cup	finely chopped onions	250 mL
3 tablespoons	lemon juice	50 mL
1 teaspoon	salt	5 mL
¼ cup	olive oil	50 mL
	Romaine lettuce leaves	

Put the bulghur in a bowl and completely cover with cold water. Leave it to soak for about 10 minutes. Drain and place on a double thickness of cheesecloth. Squeeze out moisture until dry and drop bulghur into a deep bowl.

Add to the bulghur the tomatoes, parsley, onion, lemon juice, salt and olive oil. Toss gently. Place romaine leaves on a serving platter or line a bowl with them. Mound the mixture on top of the romaine.

Serves 4

HINT: To keep herbs such as parsley fresh, place the stems in a glass of water in the refrigerator and snip from the "bouquet" as needed.

Heart of Palm Salad

A truly elegant salad.

¼ cup	vegetable oil	50 mL
2 tablespoons	red wine vinegar	25 mL
1 teaspoon	sugar	5 mL
½ teaspoon	salt	2 mL
¼ teaspoon	pepper	1 mL
2	cans heart of palm (each 14 oz./398 mL)	2
1	can artichoke hearts (14 oz./398 mL)	1
3	tomatoes	3
1	head lettuce or chicory	1

In a medium bowl, mix together the oil, vinegar, sugar, salt and pepper. Drain the heart of palm and cut into 1-inch (2.5 cm) pieces. Drain the artichoke hearts and cut into bite-sized pieces. Cut the tomatoes into large pieces. Add the heart of palm, artichokes and tomatoes to the dressing and toss to coat well.

Tear the lettuce into pieces and arrange on a platter. Spoon the mixture over it. Serve chilled.

Serves 4 to 6

Heart of palm are tender, ivory-coloured shoots of palm from the core at the top of the palm tree. They can be used in salads or served warm like asparagus. They are available, canned, in specialty food stores.

Café Salad

Years ago I ordered a salad for lunch in a restaurant in Ottawa. It was quite unusual and tasted great, so I picked through the dish, writing down the ingredients that I could identify. At home I tried to replicate it. This is as close as I could come going by memory, as the restaurant closed down shortly after.

1 pound	fresh spinach	500 g
½	cucumber, sliced and quartered	½
1	carrot, chopped	1
½	green pepper, chopped	½
3	green onions, chopped	3
1	celery stalk, sliced	1
1	tomato, sliced and quartered	1
1 cup	sliced radicchio	250 mL
	Alfalfa sprouts	
¼ cup	salad oil	50 mL
1 tablespoon	red wine vinegar	15 mL
1 tablespoon	sugar	15 mL
1 teaspoon	curry powder	5 mL

Clean and dry the spinach thoroughly. Tear into small pieces and place in a salad bowl with the rest of the vegetables.

Mix together the oil, vinegar, sugar and curry, blending well. Pour over the salad and toss well.

Serves 6

Mixed Green Salad

These are some ideas you can use to experiment and develop a salad all your own.

Bibb, Boston or romaine lettuce — Use any or all three
Spinach
Escarole — A little bit for flavour
Radicchio — A little bit for colour
Mushrooms — Try enoki, oyster or shiitake
Chopped fresh parsley, chives, tarragon — Use any or all three
Toasted sesame seeds
Fresh ground pepper
Salad dressing (see pages 165–170)

Wash the salad greens under cold running water and dry well. Tear into pieces. Place in a bowl and top with the mushrooms and seasonings. Toss well and serve with salad dressings on the side.

Escarole in a broad-leafed endive. Because of its sharp taste, it is usually used only as an accent in salads.

Radicchio is a member of the chicory family and looks like a small red cabbage. It adds colour to salads or can be used as a garnish.

Fiddlehead Salad

We have ferns growing right behind our farm house, so I make a point of going out every day when fiddleheads are in season and picking some. If cleaned thoroughly and blanched, they freeze quite well.

3 cups	fresh fiddleheads	750 mL
¼ cup	olive oil	50 mL
2 tablespoons	orange juice	25 mL
1 teaspoon	Dijon mustard	5 mL
¼ teaspoon	salt	1 mL
Pinch	pepper	Pinch
2	oranges, peeled and sectioned	2
2	green onions, chopped	2
2 tablespoons	pine nuts, toasted	25 mL

Clean as much of the brown scales as you can from the fiddleheads. Rinse thoroughly under cold running water. Add to boiling water and cook for a couple of minutes. Drain water and rinse fiddleheads. Add more water to pot, bring to a boil and add fiddleheads. This will enable you to clean them further. Cook for an additional couple of minutes until fiddleheads are tender-crisp. Drain and refresh under cold running water. Drain again.

Whisk together the oil, orange juice, mustard, salt and pepper. Add the fiddleheads and toss until well coated.

Arrange the orange sections around the edge of a platter. Mound the fiddleheads in the centre and sprinkle with the onions and toasted pine nuts.

Serves 4

Fiddleheads are the young shoots of a certain fern that are picked when they are just emerging from the ground and still tightly curled. They may be bought fresh in the spring or frozen. Once they are boiled, they can be served as a hot vegetable or chilled and added to a salad.

Greek Salad

1	head iceberg lettuce	1
½ pound	feta cheese	250 g
1	medium onion	1
1	green pepper	1
2	tomatoes, diced	2
1 cup	black Greek olives	250 mL
½ cup	olive oil	125 mL
¼ cup	red wine vinegar	50 mL
	Juice of one lemon	
1 teaspoon	crushed oregano	5 mL
½ teaspoon	salt	2 mL
	Fresh ground pepper	

Break the lettuce into cubes and place in a salad bowl. Crumble the feta, slice the onion into thin rings and slice the pepper into strips. Add to the lettuce along with the diced tomatoes and black olives.

In a separate bowl, combine the remaining ingredients. Beat until smooth. Just before serving, pour over the salad and toss until vegetables are coated.

Serves 4 to 6

Black Greek olives are very pungent and meaty, cured in brine. The Kalamata is a favourite and can be identified by its pointed bottom.

Spinach Salad with Pine Nuts

This is probably the salad we make the most often. The children love it and, though there are seldom leftovers, if there are they will keep quite well, refrigerated and covered, until the next day.

1 pound	fresh spinach	500 g
½ pound	bacon	250 g
½	head cauliflower	½
½ pound	fresh mushrooms	250 g
¼ cup	pine nuts	50 mL
¼ cup	butter	50 mL

Break the stems off the spinach and tear the leaves into large pieces. Rinse in cold water and dry thoroughly in a salad dryer or with paper towels. Place in a large bowl.

Dice the bacon and fry until crisp. Drain well and blot excess grease with paper towel. Add to the spinach.

Break the cauliflower into small flowerets and add to the spinach. Slice the mushrooms and add to the spinach mixture. Toss gently.

In a small skillet, sauté the pine nuts in the butter over low heat until lightly toasted and golden brown. Keep warm. Just before you serve the salad, pour the toasted pine nuts and warmed butter over the salad and toss gently. Serve with a creamy salad dressing.

Serves 6

Cucumber and Yogourt Salad

2	large cucumbers	2
¼ cup	finely chopped onions	50 mL
2	firm tomatoes	2
¼ cup	chopped cilantro	50 mL
1½ cups	plain yogourt	375 mL
1½ teaspoons	salt	7 mL
1 teaspoon	ground cumin	5 mL

Peel the cucumbers and halve lengthwise. Scoop out the seeds and discard. Chop the cucumber into ½-inch (1 cm) cubes and place in a bowl with the chopped onion. Cut the tomatoes into ½-inch (1 cm) cubes and add to the cucumber. Add the cilantro.

Blend the yogourt together with the salt and cumin; pour over the vegetables. Toss gently, taste for seasoning and refrigerate to chill completely.

Serves 6

Marinated Tomatoes

Slice tomatoes crosswise and place in a single layer in a deep dish. Sprinkle evenly with salt, pepper, chopped green onions and fresh or dried basil or thyme. Dried dill gives a nice flavour also. Top with a light sprinkling of wine vinegar and olive oil.

Let marinate for at least 30 minutes before serving.

This recipe also works well with sliced cucumbers instead of tomatoes.

Crab Meat Salad

1	head lettuce	1
1 pound	crab meat	500 g
1 cup	mayonnaise	250 mL
¼ cup	whipping cream	50 mL
¼ cup	chili sauce or tomato relish	50 mL
1 teaspoon	Worcestershire sauce	5 mL
¼ cup	chopped green pepper	50 mL
¼ cup	chopped green onion	50 mL
2 tablespoons	lemon juice	25 mL

Line a small bowl with large lettuce leaves and put some chopped lettuce in the bottom. Spread crab meat over the lettuce. (If using frozen crab meat, be sure it is thawed and well drained.)

In a small bowl, mix together the remaining ingredients. Pour this sauce over the crab meat and blend very slightly. Keep chilled until ready to serve.

Serves 4

Stuffed Avocado

2	large avocados, halved and pitted	2
¾ cup	chopped crab meat	175 mL
1	small onion, finely chopped	1
1	celery stalk, finely chopped	1
3 tablespoons	mayonnaise	50 mL
1 teaspoon	lemon juice	5 mL
Pinch	garlic powder	Pinch
	Salt to taste	
	Pepper to taste	

In a small bowl, blend the crab meat, onion, celery, mayonnaise and lemon juice. Add the garlic powder, salt and pepper. Place the avocado halves on individual plates and spoon the mixture into the cavity.

Serves 4

Bigard Salad Dressing

This recipe was given to my family by an old friend, Barney Bigard, clarinetist with Duke Ellington and Louis Armstrong for a number of years throughout his career.

1	egg	1
½ teaspoon	dry mustard	2 mL
½ teaspoon	salt	2 mL
	Juice of one lemon	
¼ teaspoon	garlic powder	1 mL
2	pinches cayenne pepper	2
1 cup	salad oil	250 mL

Put all the ingredients, except the salad oil, in a blender. Add ¼ cup (50 mL) of the oil and blend at high speed for 5 seconds. Take cover off and, with the blender running, gradually add remaining oil. Cover and let run for 5 seconds.

Makes 1¼ cups (300 mL)

French Dressing

1 cup	salad oil	250 mL
⅓ cup	white vinegar	75 mL
⅔ cup	sugar	150 mL
1¼ cups	chili sauce	300 mL
3	dashes Worcestershire sauce	3
1 teaspoon	finely chopped onion	5 mL
½ teaspoon	garlic salt	2 mL
½ teaspoon	celery salt	2 mL
	Salt to taste	
	Pepper to taste	

Blend all ingredients together well and add salt and pepper to taste.

Makes 3¼ cups (800 mL)

Blender Salad Dressing

1 cup	salad oil	250 mL
1 tablespoon	lemon juice	15 mL
1	garlic clove	1
½ teaspoon	salt	2 mL
¼ teaspoon	paprika	1 mL
3 oz.	Roquefort cheese	75 g

Place all ingredients in blender and blend until thoroughly mixed.

Makes 1½ cups (375 mL)

Creamy Garlic
Salad Dressing

½ cup	plain yogourt	125 mL
3 tablespoons	mayonnaise	50 mL
2 teaspoons	Dijon mustard	10 mL
¼ cup	chopped fresh parsley	50 mL
2	garlic cloves, crushed	2
	Salt to taste	
	Pepper to taste	

Mix together all the ingredients in a small bowl.

Makes about ¾ cup (175 mL)

Creamy Parmesan Salad Dressing

½ cup	sour cream	125 mL
¼ cup	salad oil	50 mL
1 tablespoon	white wine vinegar	15 mL
1	garlic clove, crushed	1
2 teaspoons	minced shallot	10 mL
¼ teaspoon	salt	1 mL
	Fresh ground pepper	
¼ cup	grated Parmesan cheese	50 mL

Mix all the ingredients together in a small bowl.

Makes 1 cup (250 mL)

Vinaigrette

1 teaspoon	salt	5 mL
¼ teaspoon	fresh ground pepper	1 mL
2 tablespoons	wine vinegar	25 mL
½ cup	oil	125 mL

Place the salt and pepper in a small bowl and add the vinegar, stirring until the salt dissolves. Stir in the oil.

Proceed with seasoning:

VARIATIONS

MUSTARD VINAIGRETTE: Add 1 teaspoon (5 mL) Dijon mustard.

GARLIC VINAIGRETTE: Add 1 crushed garlic glove. This can be put in with the salt and pepper.

ORANGE VINAIGRETTE: Add 2 tablespoons (25 mL) orange juice, a bit of grated orange peel and a pinch of sugar.

HERBED VINAIGRETTE: Use any chopped fresh herbs such as parsley, chives, basil, marjoram, tarragon. You may also add chopped shallots, capers, or a couple of tablespoons of spinach or tomato purée.

Makes ½ cup (125 mL)

HINT: When adding nuts to a salad, pasta or any other moist dish, toast them a little first. Place in a shallow pan in your oven for 10 minutes at 350°F (180°C).

Sauces

Mustard Sauce

6	egg yolks, lightly beaten	6
1 cup	vinegar	250 mL
1 cup	sugar	250 mL
½ cup	butter	125 mL
2 tablespoons	dry mustard	25 mL

Mix all ingredients together in top of a double boiler. Cook over moderate heat, stirring constantly, until mixture is thick.

Excellent with ham.

Makes 3 cups (750 mL)

Pesto Sauce

I grow basil in my garden and can hardly wait until it is ready to pick so I can make pesto. To freeze, omit cheese and add just before using.

2 cups	packed fresh basil leaves	500 mL
½ cup	olive oil	125 mL
¼ cup	pine nuts or walnuts	50 mL
2	garlic cloves, crushed	2
¼ teaspoon	salt	1 mL
½ cup	grated Parmesan cheese	125 mL

Combine all ingredients except Parmesan in food processor and blend on high speed until mixture forms a well-mixed paste. Transfer to a bowl and stir in cheese. Store, covered, in refrigerator.

Stir a little into soup, hot cooked vegetables or rice. Good on broiled steaks and baked potatoes.

Toss hot drained pasta with butter. Thoroughly mix pesto sauce into it and serve.

Makes 1¾ cups (425 mL)

HINT: To prevent pesto from darkening, reserve 1 tablespoon (15 mL) of the oil required in the recipe. Place the pesto in a jar with a tight-fitting lid and pour the reserved oil on the top, forming a seal. Stir the oil into the sauce before using.

Steak Marinade

This is excellent to use on a cut of meat that you think may be tough or lack flavour. I have used it to salvage the most hopeless steaks imaginable.

1 cup	soya sauce	250 mL
2	large onions, coarsely chopped	2
2	garlic cloves, halved	2
¼ cup	bottled gravy colouring	50 mL
2 teaspoons	Beau Monde Seasoning	10 mL

Combine soya sauce, onion and garlic in blender and process at high speed until smooth. Blend in gravy colouring and Beau Monde Seasoning. Bottle and store in refrigerator. It will last forever.

Brush on steak and marinate for 2 hours.

Beau Monde Seasoning is a commercially prepared blend of seasonings. It can be found in spice racks in specialty food stores and in some supermarkets.

Salsa

Salsa is the Spanish word for "sauce". It is a condiment containing tomatoes, chilies, onions, cilantro, garlic and seasonings, and it's commonly used as a topping for nachos and tacos.

2	large tomatoes, chopped	2
1 cup	chopped onion	250 mL
2	garlic cloves, minced	2
2	serrano or jalapeño chilies, seeded and finely chopped	2
2 tablespoons	chopped fresh cilantro	25 mL
1 tablespoon	chopped fresh basil	15 mL
2 tablespoons	lemon or lime juice	25 mL
½ teaspoon	sugar	2 mL
	Salt to taste	

Mix all the ingredients together in a bowl and let stand for a couple of hours for the flavours to blend. Store, covered, in refrigerator. Use with nachos or on the side with seafood.

Makes about 2 cups (500 mL)

Jalapeño chilies are dark green and about 2 inches (5 cm) long with a rounded end. They are extremely hot. Buy them fresh or in canned or pickled form.

Serrano chilies are green, long and thin. They are very hot and can be found fresh or canned.

Mayonnaise

I have been making my own mayonnaise for years. It is quick and easy and much more economical than store-bought. Experiment with different mustards and seasonings. Tarragon gives it a tangy flavour.

2	eggs	2
1½ teaspoons	salt	7 mL
1 teaspoon	Dijon mustard	5 mL
¼ cup	lemon juice	50 mL
2 cups	vegetable oil	500 mL

Place all ingredients, except oil, in blender. Add about 1 cup (250 mL) oil and start blender on low. Increase to medium-high and slowly pour in remaining oil. Continue until completely blended and thick. Pour into storage container and keep refrigerated for no more than two weeks. (Ours has never been around any longer than that.)

Makes about 2¼ cups (550 mL)

Green Peppercorn Sauce

1 tablespoon	green peppercorns	15 mL
½ cup	mayonnaise	125 mL
1 teaspoon	lemon juice	5 mL

Place peppercorns in a blender or food processor and flash on and off until peppercorns are slightly broken. Add mayonnaise and lemon juice; process until well blended. Keep refrigerated. You may serve immediately, but the flavour will be better after a day or so.

Excellent with beef and seafood.

Makes ½ cup (125 mL)

Skordalia
(Garlic Potato Sauce)

Make sure everyone has some Skordalia, as there is quite a bit of garlic in it and those who don't have any won't be able to talk with those who do!

1	large potato, peeled	1
1 tablespoon	minced garlic	15 mL
1 teaspoon	salt	5 mL
1	egg yolk	1
6 tablespoons	olive oil	90 mL
2 tablespoons	lemon juice	25 mL
	Fresh ground pepper	
	Salt	

Cut the potato into small cubes and boil in salted water until completely cooked. Drain and return potatoes to the pot. Shake over moderate heat until dry. Mash well.

Mash the garlic and salt together to make a paste. Add to the potatoes and blend in well. Beat in the egg yolk. Add the oil, a tablespoon (15 mL) at a time, until it is all absorbed. Beat in the lemon juice and season to taste with pepper and salt. If the sauce is too thick, beat in a little warm water until you achieve the desired consistency.

Excellent with grilled or fried seafood.

Makes 1 cup (250 mL)

Tzatziki
(Cucumber Sauce)

1 cup	yogourt	250 mL
1	garlic clove, crushed	1
2 tablespoons	grated cucumber	25 mL
	Salt and pepper	

Place the yogourt in a small bowl and add the crushed garlic clove and the cucumber. Mix well. Season to taste. Keep refrigerated.

Serve on the side as a sauce for meat.

Makes 1 cup (250 mL)

Rémoulade

1 cup	mayonnaise	250 mL
1 tablespoon	Dijon mustard	15 mL
Dash	hot pepper sauce	Dash
2	green onions, minced, including 1 inch (2.5 cm) of green tops	2
1 tablespoon	chopped fresh parsley (or 1 teaspoon/5 mL dried)	15 mL
1 tablespoon	chopped fresh chives (or 1 teaspoon/5 mL dried)	15 mL
½ teaspoon	dried chervil	2 mL
¼ teaspoon	dried tarragon	1 mL
Pinch	cayenne pepper	Pinch
1	anchovy fillet, minced	1
1 tablespoon	drained crushed capers	15 mL

Combine all of the ingredients and blend well. Keep refrigerated.

Rémoulade makes a wonderful dip with shellfish. It can also be served with cold meat and poultry.

Makes 1¼ cups (300 mL)

Cocktail Sauce

1 tablespoon	butter	15 mL
1 tablespoon	minced onion	15 mL
1	garlic clove, crushed	1
½ cup	water	125 mL
⅓ cup	tomato paste	75 mL
1 teaspoon	lemon juice	5 mL
1 tablespoon	horseradish	15 mL
¼ teaspoon	salt	1 mL
½ teaspoon	dry mustard	2 mL
¼ teaspoon	cayenne pepper	1 mL

Melt the butter in a small saucepan and cook the onion and garlic until tender. Mix in the remaining ingredients and bring to a boil. Reduce heat and simmer for about 10 minutes, until thick. May be served warm or chilled.

Use as a dipping sauce for seafood.

Makes about 1 cup (250 mL)

Peanut Sauce

This is a Thai recipe that makes a great dip for satay. Be frugal with the chili flakes or it will be quite hot.

1	small onion, chopped	1
2 tablespoons	peanut oil	25 mL
1 tablespoon	soya sauce	15 mL
1½ teaspoons	lime juice	7 mL
½ teaspoon	grated lime peel	2 mL
¼ teaspoon	crushed dried chili flakes	1 mL
1 teaspoon	sugar	5 mL
1	garlic clove, minced	1
¼ cup	peanut butter	50 mL
½ cup	coconut milk or table cream	125 mL

Mix together all of the ingredients, except the coconut milk, in a food processor and process until smooth. While blending, add enough of the coconut milk to make a thin dipping consistency. Refrigerate until ready to serve.

Makes 1 cup (250 mL)

Coconut milk is not the liquid found inside a coconut. It can be bought in cans from specialty food stores and most supermarkets.

Desserts

Baked Whole Pineapple

1	whole pineapple	1
20	whole cloves	20
½ cup	maple syrup	125 mL
1 teaspoon	ground cinnamon	5 mL
	Ice cream	
	Maraschino cherries	

Completely pare the outside off the pineapple. Remove the eyes and insert whole cloves in the holes. Insert the rotisserie spit through the pineapple. You may have to use a skewer to make the hole first. Secure with holding forks.

Place on the rotisserie and rotate over medium heat, with the lid partway up, until tender. This is the preferred method, but you may also place on the upper grill over medium heat, turning frequently.

Baste frequently with a mixture of the maple syrup and cinnamon.

Cooking Time: 30 to 40 minutes

When pineapple is completely cooked, remove it from the spit. Slice it lengthwise down the middle and lay open on a platter. Cut into ½-inch (1 cm) slices.

To serve, place 2 pineapple slices on each plate with a scoop of ice cream in the middle and a Maraschino cherry on top.

Serves 6

Empanadas

A dessert from sunny Mexico.

2 cups	flour	500 mL
½ teaspoon	salt	2 mL
1 tablespoon	sugar	15 mL
1 teaspoon	baking powder	5 mL
½ cup	shortening	125 mL
⅓ cup	ice water	75 mL
	Oil for deep-frying	
	Fillings: applesauce, crushed pineapple, custard, fruit jams	

Combine the flour, salt, sugar and baking powder; blend together well. Cut in the shortening with a pastry blender until mixture resembles fine meal. Add water and mix into a firm dough. Form into 16 balls and roll out on a lightly floured board to make 4-inch (10 cm) circles.

Place a spoonful of filling on one half of each pastry circle. Moisten the edges with water and fold over the other side, pressing the edges together to seal.

Deep-fry in hot oil until golden brown or place on cookie sheet on upper grill over medium-low heat. If baking, prick the tops with a fork before putting in the barbecue. If you like, while they are still hot, sprinkle them with sugar.

Cooking Time: 10 to 15 minutes

Serves 8

Bananas au Rhum

A quick and easy dessert that's as tasty as it is elegant.

4	bananas	4
	Lemon juice	
¼ cup	butter	50 mL
½ cup	brown sugar	125 mL
	Cinnamon	
3 tablespoons	rum	50 mL
	Vanilla ice cream	

Peel the bananas and sprinkle all over with lemon juice to prevent darkening.

Melt the butter in a skillet over medium heat and mix in the brown sugar. Add the bananas, turning to coat evenly. Cook for 3 or 4 minutes and sprinkle with cinnamon.

Warm the rum in a small saucepan. Pour over the bananas and ignite with a match. When flame dies down, serve bananas over vanilla ice cream with sauce drizzled over top.

Serves 4

Crêpes

I usually make more crêpes than I need, wrap them up well and keep on hand in the freezer. Crêpes have a multitude of uses, as you can stuff them with just about everything imaginable: creamed seafoods, vegetables, fruits, cheeses, ice cream . . . the list is endless. You could make a whole meal out of crêpes!

½ cup	butter	125 mL
½ cup	cold water	125 mL
¼ cup	milk	50 mL
2	eggs	2
2	egg yolks	2
¾ cup	flour	175 mL
1 tablespoon	sugar	15 mL
2 tablespoons	cognac	25 mL

Melt the butter and place 2 tablespoons (25 mL) in a blender. Add the remaining ingredients and blend well. Let rest for a couple of hours.

Heat an 8-inch (20 cm) skillet over moderately high heat and brush pan with melted butter. Pour in ¼ cup (50 mL) batter and rotate quickly to spread batter evenly. Brown on both sides until golden. Remove and stack with waxed paper in between.

These will keep, refrigerated, for a few days. You may also freeze them.

Makes 12 to 16

Crêpes Suzette

On numerous occasions I have embarrassed myself by pigging out on Crêpes Suzette in front of guests. I will continue to eat them until there are no more left, hoping that no one will accept when I offer seconds!

12	prepared crêpes (page 187)	12
⅓ cup	orange juice	75 mL
¼ cup	butter	50 mL
2 tablespoons	sugar	25 mL
1 teaspoon	grated orange peel	5 mL
¼ cup	orange liqueur	50 mL

About 20 minutes before serving, start to prepare the orange sauce. In a 10-inch (25 cm) skillet over low heat on the lower grill, warm the orange juice, butter, sugar and orange peel until the butter melts. Fold the crêpes in quarters, arrange in the sauce and heat through, spooning the sauce over them.

In a small saucepan over medium heat, heat the liqueur until hot. Remove from heat and pour over the crêpes. Ignite immediately with a match. Serve when the flame dies down.

Serves 6

Ice Cream Crêpes

A simple and elegant dessert that can be prepared well in advance.

12	prepared crêpes (page 187)	12
	Strawberry ice cream	
½ cup	blanched sliced almonds	125 mL
1 cup	sugar	250 mL
⅔ cup	cocoa powder	150 mL
⅓ cup	butter	75 mL
½ cup	milk	125 mL
½ cup	corn syrup	125 mL
½ teaspoon	almond extract	2 mL

Chill prepared crêpes in refrigerator. Chill a large cookie sheet in freezer.

Cover cookie sheet with waxed paper. Spoon ice cream on the centre of each crepe and fold over the two sides so they overlap. Place on cookie sheet and put in freezer until firm. Cover them if you are not going to use them the same day.

Toast the almonds in a small skillet over medium heat until lightly browned, stirring often. Set aside.

In a medium saucepan over medium heat, cook the sugar, cocoa, butter, milk and corn syrup until smooth, stirring often. Bring to a boil, remove from heat and add almond extract.

Pour warm chocolate sauce over crêpes and sprinkle with toasted almonds.

Serve immediately.

Serves 8 to 12

HINT: For easy measuring of honey, corn syrup or molasses, lightly coat the cup or spoon with vegetable oil.

Celestial Cheesecake

I am a great cheesecake fan, probably because they are not too sweet. Use your imagination to come up with some different toppings such as fresh fruit, sauces and glazes.

¾ cup	butter	175 mL
1¼ cups	flour	300 mL
2 cups	sugar	500 mL
3	egg yolks	3
	Grated peel of two lemons	
5	packages cream cheese (each 8 oz./250 g)	5
3 tablespoons	flour	50 mL
5	eggs	5
¼ cup	milk	50 mL

With mixer at low speed, beat the butter, 1¼ cups (300 mL) flour, ¼ cup sugar (50 mL), 1 egg yolk and half of the grated lemon peel until well mixed. Shape into a ball and wrap in waxed paper. Chill for 1 hour.

Press one-third of the dough into bottom — not sides — of a 10-inch (3 L) springform pan. Bake at 400°F (200°C) for 8 minutes. Cool.

With mixer at medium speed, in a large bowl beat the cream cheese until smooth. Slowly beat in 1¾ cups (425 mL) sugar. At low speed, beat in 3 tablespoons (50 mL) flour, the remaining egg yolks and lemon peel, the eggs and milk. Beat for 5 minutes at medium speed.

Press rest of dough around side of pan. Pour in cream cheese mixture. Bake at 475°F (240°C) for 12 minutes. Reduce heat to 300°F (150°C) and bake for 35 minutes longer. Turn off oven and let cheesecake remain in oven for 30 minutes. Be sure cake is firm in centre. Remove from oven and cool in pan on wire rack.

Remove pan side and carefully transfer cheescake to a platter. Top with fresh fruit or a glaze. Store in refrigerator.

HINT: When making cheesecake, a couple of cracks are normal. Really deep cracks indicate that the cake has cooked too long or at too high a temperature. Exposure to drafts when cooling can also cause cracks. Loosen cake from sides of pan so it can contract easily as it cools.

Strawberry Cheese Tart

This is, without a doubt, my favourite pie. Whenever I see fresh strawberries, I picture Strawberry Cheese Tart. It is also the most attractive pie you could serve.

One 9-inch (23 cm) baked pastry shell, cooled		
3 oz.	cream cheese, softened	75 g
3 tablespoons	sour cream	50 mL
1½ quarts	strawberries	1.5 L
1 cup	sugar	250 mL
3 tablespoons	cornstarch	50 mL
Red food colouring		

In a small bowl, beat the cream cheese until fluffy. Add the sour cream and beat until smooth. Spread in the cooled pie shell and refrigerate. Wash and hull the berries. Pick out enough of the nicest ones to cover the top of the pie and set aside.

Mash enough remaining strawberries to make up 1 cup (250 mL). Force these through a sieve and add water to make 1 cup (250 mL). In a medium saucepan, off the stove, mix together the sugar and cornstarch. Add ½ cup (125 mL) water and the sieved berries. Cook over moderate heat, stirring, until the mixture is clear and thickened. Boil for about 1 minute. Remove from heat, stir to cool slightly and add a little red food colouring until the sauce is ruby red. Fill the pie shell with the remaining berries, tips up, and pour the cooked mixture over top. Chill for 1 hour before serving.

Serves 6

HINT: To store fresh strawberries, empty them from their carton and place in a single layer in a shallow pan. It's then easy to spot any soft ones and eat them right away. Keep covered and chilled.

Daiquiri Cheesecake

⅓ cup	butter	75 mL
1⅓ cups	graham wafer crumbs	325 mL
¼ cup	sugar	50 mL
1	envelope unflavoured gelatin	1
½ cup	sugar	125 mL
⅓ cup	light rum	75 mL
½ cup	lime juice	125 mL
1 teaspoon	grated lime rind	5 mL
1 teaspoon	grated lemon rind	5 mL
4	eggs, separated	4
1 pound	cream cheese	500 g
½ cup	confectioner's sugar	125 mL
1 cup	whipping cream	250 mL

Melt butter and stir in graham wafer crumbs and ¼ cup (50 mL) sugar. Grease a 9-inch (2.5 L) springform pan. Press mixture into bottom and halfway up sides of pan. Bake at 375°F (190°C) for 8 minutes. Cool before filling.

In a medium saucepan, combine the gelatin, ½ cup (125 mL) sugar, rum and lime juice. Stir in the lime and lemon rinds. Add the egg yolks, blending well. Cook over moderate heat, stirring constantly until mixture thickens. Remove from heat and set aside to cool.

In a large mixing bowl, beat the cream cheese until light and fluffy. Add the gelatin mixture to the cream cheese and blend well.

Beat the egg whites until they form soft peaks. Slowly add the confectioner's sugar and continue beating until they form stiff peaks. Fold the egg whites into the cream cheese mixture.

Whip the cream until it is stiff, then fold into the cheese mixture. Pour mixture into the prepared crust and chill for 4 hours or until set.

Key Lime Pie

I am often able to get a basket of limes that have a few brown spots at a greatly reduced price. I squeeze the juice into jars, grate the rind into small freezer bags and freeze the whole lot for future pies.

One 9-inch (23 cm) baked pie shell		
4	eggs, separated	4
1	can sweetened condensed milk (10 oz./284 mL)	1
½ cup	lime juice	125 mL
1 teaspoon	grated lime peel	5 mL
6 tablespoons	sugar	90 mL
½ teaspoon	cream of tartar	2 mL

Beat the egg yolks. Add the condensed milk, lime juice and grated peel; beat until thick. Beat one egg white until stiff and fold into the lime mixture. Pour into the pie shell. Bake at 350°F (180°C) for 10 or 15 minutes or until the filling is firm. Let cool.

Beat the remaining egg whites until stiff, adding the sugar gradually. Add the cream of tartar and continue beating until it forms peaks. Mound this meringue on top of the pie. Bake at 450°F (230°C) for about 10 minutes, watching it carefully, until the meringue is golden brown on top.

HINT: To separate an egg efficiently, break it gently into a kitchen funnel. The yolk will remain in the funnel while the white slips through.

Pecan Pie

Serve this as the finishing touch to a Cajun meal for real authenticity.

One 9-inch (23 cm) pie shell, unbaked		
½ cup	brown sugar	125 mL
½ cup	butter, melted	125 mL
3	eggs, well beaten	3
½ teaspoon	salt	2 mL
1 cup	corn syrup	250 mL
½ cup	milk	125 mL
½ teaspoon	vanilla extract	2 mL
½ cup	finely chopped pecans	125 mL
1 cup	whipped cream	250 mL
½ cup	pecan halves	125 mL

In a medium bowl, combine the sugar, butter, eggs, salt, corn syrup and milk. Mix well with an electric beater. When blended, stir in vanilla and chopped pecans.

Pour into pie shell and bake at 350°F (180°C) for 40 or 50 minutes or until filling is set. Top with whipped cream and pecan halves.

HINT: If you don't have a nut chopper, fill a plastic bag with nuts and roll with a rolling pin.

Watermelon Basket

A Watermelon Basket is an excellent dessert for large gatherings, and it provides an attractive centrepiece for your table at the same time. The basket is impressive and you can do most of the preparation the day before.

1	large watermelon	1
2 cups	strawberries	500 mL
2 cups	raspberries	500 mL
1 cup	blueberries	250 mL
1 cup	seedless grapes	250 mL
3	bananas, sliced	3
3	oranges, sectioned	3
¾ cup	water	175 mL
1 cup	sugar	250 mL
2 cups	dry vermouth	500 mL
½ cup	Anisette	125 mL

With the tip of a very sharp knife, score a 2-inch-wide (5 cm) band across the centre of the watermelon, stopping one-third of the way down from the top. This will be the handle of the basket. Score the sides of the melon into scallops, one-third of the way down, working your way from one side of the handle to the other. When this is completed, cut through the score marks and very carefully separate the top and bottom pieces.

Hollow out the melon in large pieces and, with a melon-baller, scoop out balls and place in a large bowl. Add the rest of the fruit to the watermelon balls.

In a small saucepan, dissolve the sugar in the water over low heat. Increase the heat to moderately high and boil syrup for 5 minutes. Let cool and add the dry vermouth and Anisette. Pour the syrup over the fruit and toss lightly. Transfer the fruits to the watermelon basket and chill. Sprinkle with more Anisette just before serving. Serve on a chilled platter.

HINT: When washing strawberries, leave the hulls on to save the juice. Place berries in a colander and let a gentle spray of cold water wash over them. Remove the hulls later.

Strawberry Shortcake

This recipe is a quick and easy way to glorify fresh strawberries when the season is upon us.

2 cups	flour	500 mL
1 tablespoon	baking powder	15 mL
3 tablespoons	sugar	50 mL
½ teaspoon	salt	2 mL
½ cup	shortening	125 mL
1	egg, slightly beaten	1
½ cup	milk	125 mL
1 pint	strawberries	500 mL
2 tablespoons	sugar	25 mL
2 cups	whipping cream	500 mL
1 teaspoon	sugar	5 mL

Combine flour, baking powder, 3 tablespoons (50 mL) sugar, salt, shortening, egg and milk; beat together until just blended. Place in two greased 8-inch (1.2 L) round cake pans. Bake at 450°F (230°C) for 10 to 12 minutes. Don't be concerned if you think the mixture is too thick. That's the way it's supposed to be, heavy and gooey. Also, don't expect the cake to rise too much. It's not meant to.

When the cake has cooled, place one layer on a platter and cover with sliced strawberries, reserving some whole ones to decorate the top.

Sprinkle 2 tablespoons (25 mL) sugar over the berries. Whip the cream with 1 teaspoon (5 mL) sugar until it stands in soft peaks. Spread half of it over the strawberries. Place the second cake layer on top of the berries and cream. Spread the rest of the whipped cream over the top of the cake and decorate with whole strawberries.

HINT: If you are whipping cream ahead of time, add a pinch of unflavoured gelatin to the cream before it is whipped. This will prevent it from "weeping".

Sabayon

This is the perfect finishing touch for a rather large meal, light and not too filling. It is also a good recipe when you would like to serve dessert but don't have the time or the ingredients for most things.

4	egg yolks	4
⅓ cup	icing sugar	75 mL
⅓ cup	orange juice	75 mL

In a small bowl, beat the egg yolks and icing sugar together until they turn very light yellow. This should take about 5 minutes. Pour this into the top of a double boiler over lightly boiling water. Beat with a wire whisk while gradually pouring in the orange juice. Continue to beat for another 5 minutes until the sauce has thickened.

Pour into two dishes and serve warm. It may also be served slightly chilled.

You might want to decorate the rim of the dishes with a couple of orange slices. Cut them in half with a slit in the middle. You may also dip the edges of the orange slices in sugar.

Serves 2

HINT: Place a few marbles in the bottom of a double boiler so that when the water gets too low, the racket they make will get your attention.

Strawberry Sorbet

Sorbet is a French sherbet, often served between courses to cleanse the palate, or as a dessert.

1 cup	water	250 mL
1	envelope unflavoured gelatin	1
1	package frozen strawberries (19 oz./540 mL)	1
½ cup	corn syrup	125 mL
⅓ cup	orange liqueur	75 mL
2 tablespoons	lemon juice	25 mL

Boil water and pour into a small bowl. Sprinkle the gelatin over the water and let sit for 10 minutes. Stir until gelatin is dissolved.

In a food processor, purée the strawberries. Mix all ingredients together in a large bowl. Pour into a 9-inch square (2.5 L) dish and freeze for about 3 hours, stirring occasionally. Return mixture to large bowl and beat with electric mixer until smooth but still frozen. Return to freezer for another 2 hours before serving.

Serves 8

Cranberry Cream

A light and easy dessert you can make well in advance. Perfect for summer.

2 cups	cranberries	500 mL
¾ cup	water	175 mL
¾ cup	sugar	175 mL

OR

1	can cranberries (14 oz./398 mL)	1
1 tablespoon	unflavoured gelatin	15 mL
¼ cup	orange juice	50 mL
1 cup	whipping cream	250 mL

Combine the cranberries, water and sugar in a large saucepan and simmer for 5 minutes. Transfer to a blender and process until liquid. Return mixture to saucepan.

If using canned cranberries, process in blender and place in saucepan.

Soften the gelatin in the orange juice. Bring the cranberry mixture to a boil and add the gelatin and orange juice. Stir until dissolved. Remove from heat, let cool and then chill.

When the cranberry mixture begins to set, whip the cream and fold in gently. Pour into a serving bowl and chill for 2 hours before serving.

Serves 4

Menu Plans

A Surf 'n' Turf meal. Great for summer or, if you have the winter blahs, have a "Wish I Was in Florida" dinner.

Shrimp Coquille
Sesame Sirloin
Stuffed Baked Potatoes with Bacon and Cheese
Spinach Salad with Pine Nuts
Key Lime Pie

An elegant meal that takes a little bit of preparation.

Rumaki
Hawaiian Stuffed Chicken Breasts
Saffron Rice
Garbanzos with Pimiento
Heart of Palm Salad
Daiquiri Cheesecake

A bit of Italy.

Bruschetta
Pork Tenderloin with Mango Sauce
Orzo and Rice Amandine
Stuffed Tomatoes
Cucumber and Yogourt Salad
Strawberry Sorbet

Spend a night in the Mediterranean, without much fuss. Some of the dishes aren't Mediterranean but they do go well together.

Lime Chicken Satay with Tzatziki
Lamb Roast Stuffed with Indian Rice
Kohlrabi in Dill Sauce
Greek Salad
Cranberry Cream

Treat your guests or your family to some unusual dishes!

Baked Brie
Monkfish in Caper Sauce
Seasoned Rice with Pine Nuts
Chinese Long Beans
Marinated Tomatoes
Sabayon

This is a food extravaganza that will have everyone begging for more.

Calamari (Squid) with Skordalia
Seafood Brochettes
Florentine Rice
Sesame Broccoli
Almond Orange Salad
Strawberry Cheese Tart

You can prepare all of these dishes in advance and then sit back and enjoy the fun.

Curried Chicken Rolls
Leg of Lamb Seasoned with Herbs
Sliced Baked Potatoes with Herbs and Cheese
Baked Green Tomatoes
Tabbouleh
Strawberry Shortcake

A trip to the Far East without the expense.

Pork Satay with Peanut Sauce
Asian Quail
Pilaf
Asparagus with Saffron
Thai Cucumber Salad
Bananas au Rhum

The meal I would order in a fine dining room if they had all these dishes!

Oysters Rockefeller
Grilled Roast of Beef
Parisienne Potatoes
Cognac Carrots
Café Salad
Crêpes Suzette

A hearty meal for those with big appetites.

Escargots à la Bourguignonne
Stuffed Pork Loin Roast with Clove-Orange Baste
Scalloped Potatoes
Green Beans Amandine
Mixed Green Salad
Pecan Pie

Glossary

ANCHOVIES — Tiny fish of the herring family, used almost exclusively in preserved form, salted or pickled and packed in oil. Use sparingly as they are quite salty. Can be bought flat, rolled or in paste. Use in salads, sauces, on pizza.

BEAU MONDE SEASONING — A commercial blend of seasonings. Found in spice racks in specialty food stores.

BULGHUR (cracked wheat) — Wheat that has been cracked by boiling and then dried again. Used most often in Middle Eastern cooking.

CAPERS — Pickled buds of the caper shrub grown in the Mediterranean. Excellent with fish and sauces. Can be found, bottled, in specialty food stores or gourmet sections of supermarkets.

CAYENNE PEPPER — Made from ground red chili peppers and sometimes called red pepper. It is very hot and should be used sparingly. Used in Cajun and Mexican dishes. Not to be confused with paprika, which is much milder and made from sweet red peppers.

CHERVIL — A slight licorice flavour marks this relative of the parsley family. Frequently used in French cooking.

CHILIES
— Jalapeño — Dark green and about 2 inches (5 cm) long with a rounded end. They are extremely hot. Can be found fresh, canned or pickled.
— Serrano — Green, long and thin. They are very

hot. Can be found fresh or canned.

CILANTRO (fresh coriander) — Known by both names. Parsley can be used as a substitute, though the taste is quite different. Essential ingredient of many Asian dishes. Coriander is also available ground and as seeds.

COCONUT MILK — This is not the liquid found inside a coconut. It can be bought in cans from specialty food stores and some supermarkets.

CUMIN — A spice often used in Indian curry, it resembles caraway. Available ground or in seeds.

ENGLISH CUCUMBER — A long, thinner cucumber with fewer and smaller seeds.

ESCAROLE — A broad-leafed endive. Because of its sharp taste, it is usually used only as an accent in salads.

FETA CHEESE — A curd goat cheese, traditionally from Greece. Stored in water, which must be drained off.

FIDDLEHEADS — Young ferns. They are picked when they are just emerging from the ground and still tightly curled. May be bought fresh in the spring or frozen. Once they are boiled, they can be served as a hot vegetable or chilled and added to a salad.

FISH SAUCE — Made from the liquid drained from salted, fermented anchovies. Use sparingly. It is an essential ingredient in the cooking of some Asian countries. Can be found in Asian and specialty food stores.

GARAM MASALA — A combination of ground spices including cardamom, cinnamon, cloves, coriander, cumin and nutmeg. Used in Indian cooking and available on spice racks in specialty food stores.

GARBANZOS (chick peas) — Most often used in Middle Eastern cooking. Can be found canned in most supermarkets. Also available dried, but must be soaked and boiled in water until tender.

GINGER (fresh) — A perennial root often used in Oriental cooking. Once the skin has been scraped away, it can be chopped, sliced or grated. Also available candied and ground.

GREEK OLIVES — The Greek black is very pungent and meaty, cured in brine. The Kalamata is a favourite and can be identified by its pointed bottom.

HEART OF PALM — Tender, ivory-coloured shoots of palm from the core at the top of the palm tree. Used in salads or served warm like asparagus. Available, canned, in specialty food stores.

HOT PEPPER SAUCE — This sauce is made from chili peppers and can be very hot. Use only a few drops to season sauces. Sometimes known as Louisiana Hot Sauce.

KOHLRABI — German for "cabbage-turnip". A member of the cabbage family but milder in taste with a firm body like the turnip.

LEMON GRASS — Sold in stalks that resemble dried green onions. Must be chopped or bruised before using. Use only 6 to 8 inches (15 to 20 cm) from the base of the stalk. Can be kept in a jar of water for several weeks; change the water daily. May also be bought dried. To restore, add several pieces to a bowl of hot water for 15 minutes, then drain. Available in Oriental food stores.

LIQUID SMOKE — A mixture of water and natural liquid smoke. Adds extra barbecue flavour and can be used directly on meat or in sauces. Usually found in condiment section of food stores.

MANGO — A sturdy yellow fruit, somewhat like a peach, but with a firmer skin. Ripe mangoes have yellow to red smooth skin that yields to gentle pressure. Peel the skin from the stem end.

MUSHROOMS
— Enoki — Delicate, thin Japanese mushrooms. Do not have a strong flavour but have a crisp texture. Good for stir-fried dishes and salads. Eat raw or cook briefly.
— Oyster — Large, ruffled, whitish-gray and elegant in appearance. Good with meat, poultry and seafood. Eat raw or cook briefly.
— Shiitake — Another Japanese mushroom, which can be purchased fresh or dried.

ORZO — Pasta shaped like grains of rice.

OYSTER SAUCE — A rich brown sauce made from oysters cooked in salt and soya sauce. Can be bought in Asian and specialty food stores.

PAPAYA — A juicy fruit with smooth orange-yellow flesh. The size of a small melon, it has a similar seed-filled cavity, though it is really a berry. Purchase fruit that is greenish-yellow and yields to gentle pressure.

PHYLLO PASTRY — A paper-thin dough that makes a flaky crust. Traditionally Greek. May be bought fresh or frozen.

PINE NUTS — A small, light-coloured nut found in Italian grocery stores or specialty food stores. A delicious replacement for slivered almonds.

PRAWNS — Somewhat the same as shrimp, which may be substituted.

RADICCHIO — A member of

the chicory family but looks like a small red cabbage. Adds colour to salads.

SAFFRON — Made from the dried stamens of saffron crocus. It is the most expensive of all spices, but you need only a little bit to go a long way. It is available in threads or ground. It may be crushed or dissolved in hot liquid.

SESAME OIL — Made from roasted crushed white sesame seeds. It has a wonderful nutty flavour and is used in small quantities. Can be bought in Asian or specialty food stores and some supermarkets.

SHALLOTS — Member of the onion family. Tiny and round with a subtle taste.

SPAGHETTI SQUASH — A squash that, when cooked, comes apart in long strands of flesh.

SUN-DRIED TOMATOES — Exactly what the name says. It is necessary to blanch them in boiling water for a couple of minutes and drain well. You may do this as you need them, or do all at once and store, packed in a jar with olive oil. They may also be purchased bottled in oil. Can be found in specialty food stores and many supermarkets.

TAHINI — A paste made from ground sesame seeds. Used in Middle Eastern cooking. Available in specialty food stores.

TARRAGON — Has a slight licorice flavour. Widely used in vinegar and mustard. An essential ingredient in Béarnaise sauce and tartare sauce. Excellent in poultry, seafood, vegetables, salad dressings and sauces.

TURMERIC — A member of the ginger family and one of the principal ingredients of Indian curry powder. It is not hot, but has a pronounced flavour and adds a yellow colouring to food.

Index

Almond Orange Salad, 153
Antipasta, 38
Appetizers — Artichoke
    Squares, 33
  Baked Brie, 35
  Bruschetta, 36
  Calamari (Squid), 26
  Curried Chicken Rolls, 20
  Escargots à la
    Bourguignonne, 30
  Frogs' Legs, 27
  Hot Crab Meat Dip, 28
  Lime Chicken Satay, 19
  Nachos, 37
  Oysters Bienville, 24
  Oysters Rockefeller, 22
  Pesto Mushrooms, 32
  Pizza, 39
  Pork Satay, 18
  Rumaki, 31
  Shrimp Coquille, 29
  Soft Shell Crabs with Seasoned
    Mustard Baste, 21
  Spinach Squares, 34
Artichoke Squares, 33
Artichokes — Stuffed, 118
Asian Pork Kabobs, 70
Asian Quail, 94
Asparagus with Saffron Sauce, 120
Avocado — Stuffed, 164
Bacon & Eggs in Muffin Tins, 50
Baked Brie, 35
Baked Green Tomatoes, 139
Baked Whole Pineapple, 184
Bananas au Rhum, 186

Beans — Chinese Long, 122
  Green, Amandine, 121
Beef — Blackened Steak, 59
  Feta Burgers, 64
  Grilled Roast Beef, 60
  Mexicali Burgers, 63
  Sesame Sirloin, 58
  Teriyaki, 61
  Texas Ribs, 62
Beverages — Melon Baby, 44
  Raspberry Syllabub, 46
  Slush, 42
  Strawberry Daiquiri, 45
  Verry Berry Punch, 43
Bigard Salad Dressing, 165
Blackened Steak, 59
Blender Salad Dressing, 167
Breakfast Dishes, 47
Brie — Baked, 35
Broccoli — Sesame, 123
Bruschetta, 36
Brussels Sprouts with
    Caraway, 124
Burgers — Feta, 64
  Garbanzo, 142
  Lamb, 78
  Mexicali, 63
Buttered Crumb Topping, 144
Butters — Seasoned, 109

Café Salad, 156
Calamari (Squid), 26
Carrots — Cognac, 125
Cauliflower — Orange, 126
Cheese — Baked Brie, 35

Cheesecake — Celestial, 190
  Daiquiri, 193
Chicken (see Poultry), 75
Chinese Long Beans, 122
Cocktail Sauce, 181
Cognac Carrots, 125
Cornish Hens in Lime, 93
Corn-on-the-Cob, 127
Crab — Crab Meat Salad, 163
  Hot Crab Meat Dip, 28
  Stuffed Avocado, 164
Cranberry Cream, 201
Creamy Garlic Salad Dressing, 168
Creamy Parmesan Salad
    Dressing, 169
Crêpes, 187
Crêpes — Ice Cream, 189
Crêpes Suzette, 188
Cucumber Salad — Thai, 152
Cucumber Sauce (Tzatziki), 179
Cucumber and Yogourt Salad, 161
Curried Chicken Rolls, 20

Daiquiri Cheesecake, 193
Daiquiri — Strawberry, 45
Desserts — Baked Whole
    Pineapple, 184
  Bananas au Rhum, 186
  Celestial Cheesecake, 190
  Cranberry Cream, 201
  Crêpes, 187
  Crêpes Suzette, 188
  Daiquiri Cheesecake, 193
  Empanadas, 185
  Ice Cream Crêpes, 189
  Key Lime Pie, 194
  Pecan Pie, 195
  Sabayon, 199
  Strawberry Cheese Tart, 192
  Strawberry Shortcake, 198

Strawberry Sorbet, 200
Watermelon Basket, 196
Dressings — Bigard Salad
    Dressing, 165
  Blender Salad Dressing, 167
  Creamy Garlic Salad
    Dressing, 168
  Creamy Parmesan Salad
    Dressing, 169
  French Dressing, 166
  Vinaigrette, 170

Eggs and Breakfast Dishes —
  Bacon & Eggs in Muffin Tins, 50
  Eggs au Gratin, 49
  Eggs Baked in Potato Skins, 52
  Eggs Florentine, 49
  Eggs Mornay, 48
  Green Eggs & Ham, 51
  Pancakes, 54
  Seasoned Hash Browns, 56
Empanadas, 185
Equipment and Safety, 5
Escargots à la Bourguignonne, 30

Feta Burgers, 64
Fiddlehead Salad, 158
Fish and Seafood — Calamari
    (Squid), 26
  Crab Meat Salad, 163
  Florida Shrimp, 112
  Frogs' Legs, 27
  Grilled Shellfish, 108
  Grilled Whole Lobster, 114
  Grilled Whole Salmon with
    Herbs, 96
  Hot Crab Meat Dip, 28
  Monkfish in Caper Sauce, 103
  Oysters Bienville, 24
  Oysters Rockefeller, 22

Peppered Prawns, 111
Red Snapper Stuffed with
    Seasoned Rice, 100
Scallops Wrapped in Green
    Onion, 113
Sea Bass with Dill and
    Horseradish, 102
Seafood Brochettes, 107
Seafood Jambalaya, 106
Seafood-Stuffed Flounder, 98
Shark Steaks With Garlic
    Lemon Paste, 105
Shrimp Coquille, 29
Shrimp in Shell, 110
Soft Shell Crabs with Seasoned
    Mustard Baste, 21
Sole in Parchment, 101
Stuffed Avocado, 164
Stuffed Lobster Tails, 116
Swordfish Steaks with Pesto, 104
Florentine Rice, 145
Florida Shrimp, 112
Flounder — Seafood-Stuffed, 98
French Dressing, 166
Frogs' Legs, 27
Fruit-Glazed Ham with Cloves, 73

Garbanzo Burgers, 142
Garbanzos with Pimiento, 143
Garlic Potato Sauce
    (Skordalia), 178
Garlic Salad Dressing —
    Creamy, 168
Greek Salad, 159
Green Beans Amandine, 121
Green Eggs & Ham, 51
Green Peppercorn Sauce, 177
Green Salad — Mixed, 157
Green Tomatoes — Baked, 139
Grilled Roast Beef, 60

Grilled Shellfish, 108
Grilled Whole Lobster, 114
Grilled Whole Salmon with
    Herbs, 96

Ham — Fruit-Glazed with
    Cloves, 73
    Maple Steak, 72
Hash Browns — Seasoned, 56
Hawaiian Stuffed Chicken
    Breasts, 90
Heart of Palm Salad, 155
Hot Crab Meat Dip, 28
Hot Dogs (Kids' Menu), 74

Ice Cream Crêpes, 189

Jambalaya — Seafood, 106
Japanese Chicken, 88

Kabobs — Asian Pork, 70
    Vegetable, 141
Key Lime Pie, 194
Kibbi, 76
Kids' Menu, 74
Kohlrabi in Dill Sauce, 128

Lamb — Kibbi, 76
    Lamb Burgers, 78
    Lamb Marinated in Red Wine
        and Herbs, 80
    Lamb Roast Stuffed with Indian
        Rice, 82
    Leg of Lamb Seasoned with
        Herbs, 81
    Rack of Lamb with Mint-
        Orange Baste, 86
    Seasoned Lamb Roast, 83
    Souvlaki, 79
Latkes, 135

Lemon Chicken, 89
Lime Chicken Satay, 19
Lobster — Grilled Whole, 114
   Stuffed Tails, 116

Maple Ham Steak, 72
Marinade — Steak, 174
Marinated Tomatoes, 162
Mayonnaise, 176
Melon Baby, 44
Mexicali Burgers, 63
Mixed Green Salad, 157
Monkfish in Caper Sauce, 103
Mushrooms — Pesto, 32
Mustard Sauce, 172

Nachos, 37

Orange Cauliflower, 126
Orzo and Rice Amandine, 147
Oysters Bienville, 24
Oysters Rockefeller, 22

Pancakes, 54
Pancakes — Potato, 135
Parisienne Potatoes, 134
Parmesan Salad Dressing —
   Creamy, 169
Peanut Sauce, 182
Pecan Pie, 195
Peppercorn Sauce — Green, 177
Peppered Prawns, 111
Peppers — Stuffed, 129
Pesto Sauce, 173
Pesto Mushrooms, 32
Pilaf, 146
Pineapple — Baked Whole, 184
Pine Nut Topping, 144
Pizza, 39
Pork — Asian Pork Kabobs, 70

Fruit-Glazed Ham with
   Cloves, 73
Kids' Menu, 74
Maple Ham Steak, 72
Pork Satay, 18
Pork Tenderloin with Mango
   Sauce, 68
Smoky Southern Ribs, 66
Stuffed Pork Loin Roast with
   Clove-Orange Baste, 71
Sweet Mustard Pork Chops, 65
Potatoes — Pancakes, 135
   Parisienne, 134
   Scalloped, 133
   Seasoned Hash Browns, 56
   Sliced Baked with Herbs and
   Cheese, 132
   Stuffed Baked with Bacon and
   Cheese, 130
Poultry — Asian Quail, 94
   Cornish Hens in Lime, 93
   Curried Chicken Rolls, 20
   Hawaiian Stuffed Chicken
   Breasts, 90
   Japanese Chicken, 88
   Lemon Chicken, 89
   Lime Chicken Satay, 19
   Spinach-Stuffed Chicken, 92
   Tandoori Chicken, 84
   Yogourt Chicken, 87
Prawns — Peppered, 111

Quail — Asian, 94

Rack of Lamb with Mint-Orange
   Baste, 86
Raspberry Syllabub, 46
Red Snapper Stuffed with
   Seasoned Rice, 100
Rémoulade, 180

Ribs — Smoky Southern, 66
  Texas, 62
Rice — Florentine, 145
  Orzo and Rice Amandine, 147
  Pilaf, 146
  Saffron, 148
  Seasoned with Pine Nuts, 150
Roast Beef — Grilled, 60
Rumaki, 31

Sabayon, 199
Saffron Rice, 148
Salads — Almond Orange, 153
  Café, 156
  Crab Meat, 163
  Cucumber and Yogourt, 161
  Fiddlehead, 158
  Greek, 159
  Heart of Palm, 155
  Marinated Tomatoes, 162
  Mixed Green, 157
  Spinach with Pine Nuts, 160
  Stuffed Avocado, 164
  Tabbouleh, 154
  Thai Cucumber, 152
Salmon — Grilled Whole with
  Herbs, 96
Salsa, 175
Satay — Lime Chicken, 19
  Pork, 18
Sauces — Cocktail, 181
  Green Peppercorn, 177
  Mayonnaise, 176
  Mustard, 172
  Peanut, 182
  Pesto, 173
  Rémoulade, 180
  Salsa, 175
  Skordalia (Garlic Potato), 178
  Steak Marinade, 174

Tzatziki (Cucumber), 179
Scalloped Potatoes, 133
Scallops Wrapped in Green
  Onion, 113
Sea Bass with Dill and
  Horseradish, 102
Seafood (see Fish and
  Seafood), 95
Seafood Brochettes, 107
Seafood Jambalaya, 106
Seafood-Stuffed Flounder, 98
Seasoned Butters, 109
Seasoned Hash Browns, 56
Seasoned Rice with Pine
  Nuts, 150
Sesame Broccoli, 123
Sesame Sirloin, 58
Shark Steaks with Garlic Lemon
  Paste, 105
Shrimp — Coquille, 29
  Florida in Shell, 112
Skordalia (Garlic Potato
  Sauce), 178
Sliced Baked Potatoes with Herbs
  and Cheese, 132
Slush, 42
Smoky Southern Ribs, 66
Soft Shell Crabs with Seasoned
  Mustard Sauce, 21
Sole in Parchment, 101
Sorbet — Strawberry, 200
Souvlaki, 79
Spaghetti Squash with
  Vegetables, 136
Spinach Salad with Pine
  Nuts, 160
Spinach Squares, 34
Spinach-Stuffed Chicken, 92
Squid (Calamari), 26
Steak — Blackened, 59

Steak Marinade, 174
Stuffed Artichokes, 118
Stuffed Avocado, 164
Stuffed Baked Potatoes with
    Bacon and Cheese, 130
Stuffed Lobster Tails, 116
Stuffed Peppers, 129
Stuffed Pork Loin Roast with
    Clove-Orange Baste, 71
Stuffed Red Snapper with
    Seasoned Rice, 100
Stuffed Tomatoes, 138
Strawberry Cheese Tart, 192
Strawberry Daiquiri, 45
Strawberry Shortcake, 198
Strawberry Sorbet, 200
Sweet Mustard Pork Chops, 65
Swordfish Steaks with Pesto, 104

Tabbouleh, 154
Tandoori Chicken, 84
Teriyaki Beef, 61
Texas Ribs, 62
Thai Cucumber Salad, 152
Tomatoes — Baked Green, 139
  Marinated, 162
  Stuffed, 138
  Tabbouleh, 154
Tzatziki (Cucumber Sauce), 179

Vegetables — Artichoke
    Squares, 33
  Artichokes — Stuffed, 118
  Asparagus with Saffron
    Sauce, 120
  Broccoli — Sesame, 123

Brussels Sprouts with
    Caraway, 124
Carrots — Cognac, 125
Cauliflower — Orange, 126
Chinese Long Beans, 122
Corn-on-the-Cob, 127
Garbanzo Burgers, 142
Garbanzos with Pimiento, 143
Green Beans Amandine, 121
Kohlrabi in Dill Sauce, 128
Mushrooms — Pesto, 32
Peppers — Stuffed, 129
Potatoes — Parisienne, 134
  Pancakes, 135
  Scalloped Potatoes, 133
  Seasoned Hash Browns, 56
  Sliced Baked with Herbs and
    Cheese, 132
  Stuffed Baked with Bacon
    and Cheese, 130
Spaghetti Squash with
    Vegetables, 136
Spinach Squares, 34
Tomatoes — Baked Green, 139
  Stuffed, 138
Vegetable Kabobs, 141
Zucchini Bake, 140
Vegetable Kabobs, 141
Verry Berry Punch, 43
Vinaigrette, 170

Watermelon Basket, 196

Yogourt Chicken, 87

Zucchini Bake, 140